MONEY MANAGEMENT DOCTRINE

Master Your Money, Master Your Life

Mithun Desai

Published by
Renu Kaul Verma
Vitasta Publishing Pvt Ltd
4348/4C, Ansari Road, Daryaganj
New Delhi - 110 002
info@vitastapublishing.com

ISBN: 978-81-19670-71-0
© Mithun Desai
First Edition 2025
MRP ₹495

All Rights Reserved.
No part of this publication may be reproduced, stored in a retrieval system, or transmitted in any form, or by any means–electronic, mechanical, photocopying, recording or otherwise–without the prior permission of the publisher. Opinions expressed in this book are the author's own. The publisher is in no way responsible for these.

Edited by Vichitra Goel
Layout by Rohit Gautam
Cover Design by Somesh Kumar Mishra
Printed at Chaman Enterprises, New Delhi

Contents

Acknowledgement ix

Preface xi

Phase: 1 Thinking   Xiii-42

1. Understanding Money
2. Set Your Goals And Objectives
3. Work Hard To Achieve Your Goals
4. Cultivate Strong Money Beliefs
5. Observe The Wealthy Around You
6. Don't Envy
7. If Others Can, So Can You
8. Wealth Is A Consequence, Not A Reward
9. Money Gets Money
10. Money Is Not A Solution

11. Money, Happiness, Price, And Value
12. Money And Mind
13. It Is Harder To Manage Yourself Than Manage Money
14. Money And/Or Passion
15. We Are Here To Make Money

Phase: 2 Becoming   43-136

16. Have A Plan
17. Have A Good Grip Over Your Finance
18. Look Wealthy, Act Wealthy, And Become Wealthy
19. Speculate To Accumulate
20. Risk Appetite
21. It's Never Late; Start Now
22. Financial Needs Are Dynamic
23. Art Of Negotiation And Deal-Making
24. Spends Less Than What You Earn
25. Don't Borrow Or Consolidate Debts
26. Understand What Is Investment
27. Build Capital And Invest Wisely
28. Equity Versus Property
29. Master The Technique Of Selling
30. Learn To Lose So You Can Win
31. Understand The Stock Market Before Buying
32. Create Multiple Streams Of Income

33. Play 'What If' To Create Wealth
34. Money Making Is Not A Secret, Learn The Art
35. Become Wealthy By Implementing
36. Listen To Your Intuition
37. Start The Investment Early
38. Work Hard To Get Rich
39. Don't Overspend, But Don't Cut Off Small Pleasures
40. Investment Is A Difficult Art
41. Working For Others Will Not Make You Rich
42. Act And Excel, Delay And Doom
43. Don't Run After Money
44. Sharpen Your Skills
45. Earning A Living Versus Making Money
46. Saving Small Or Saving Big?
47. Stick To Your Wealth Creation Plan

Phase: 3 Getting More Wealthy   137-227

48. Financial Health Check-Up
49. Money Mentor
50. Intuition
51. Strike, Attack!
52. Delegate
53. Are You A Solopreneur Or A Team Player
54. Hidden Opportunities, Hidden Assets

55. Slow And Steady Wins The Race

56. Beware Of Intruders

57. Your Money Should Work For You

58. Master The Art Of Exiting From An Investment

59. Know What Type Of Investor You Are

60. Dancing With The Financial Statements

61. It's All About Taxes

62. Assets—Make Them Work For You!

63. Know Your Worth

64. Think Out Of The Box

65. You Are Rich As It Is Your Right To Be Rich

66. Securing Your Legacy

67. Balancing Wealth And Health

68. Cultivate A Healthy Relationship With Money

69. Celebrate The Success

70. Let's Continue Our Journey Towards Financial Freedom Lifestyle

Phase: 4 Be Wealthy, As Always   228-275

71. It's All About Quality

72. Don't Be Lazy; Be Very Lazy

73. Deep Dive Into The Details

74. Spend Only 80 Per Cent Of What You Have

75. Own The Ownership

76. Preserve For The Old Age
77. The Contingency Fund
78. Understand Terminal Value Investing
79. Interesting Money Rules
80. Teach Your Children How To Create And Protect Wealth
81. What Are You Paying, What Are You Getting
82. Don't Give Equity
83. Don't Borrow From Friends And Relatives
84. Go Beyond Wealth

Phase: 5 Purpose Of Wealth Before And After   276-326

85. Before Wealth
86. After Wealth
87. Become Wealth Wise
88. Explain Poverty To Children
89. Choose Charities Wisely
90. Spend Your Money Wisely
91. Don't Lend Money To Friends And Family
92. Don't Lend, Buy Equities
93. Bonding Of Wealth
94. Be Assertive; When You Are Wealthy
95. Give With No Strings Attached
96. Take Advice From Those Who Take Responsibility

97. Don't Flaunt Your Wealth
98. Charitable Giving Versus Impact Investing
99. Why You Should Share Your Wealth
100. Legacy Wealth Sustainable Doctrines For Generations.

Acknowledgements

This book is the result of observing my father who has helped his clients create wealth in a unique way—by tax planning, fund flow planning, and following strict compliances.

As a financial professional, I've had the privilege to meet, observe and interact with many wealthy clients, fund managers, financial experts, and individuals who have created, managed, and increased their wealth wisely, in a disciplined and ethical manner.

I am thankful to my father and all the above-mentioned people, because of them I could learn the basics of the Money Management Doctrine which I am presenting here.

I would like to express my sincere gratitude to Rajesh Desai, Director of Harmony Multimedia, for his invaluable contributions in enhancing my communication skills, enabling me to convey complex ideas with simplicity and effectiveness.

Preface

All of us want to be rich, and amass wealth. But, we also know that it is easier said than done.

It leads us to ponder—is wealth creation a Science or an Art? Is it some kind of sorcery or a magic trick?

This question always hammered my mind, and to find my answer, I started talking to the wealthy to understand:
- How did they create wealth?
- How do they spend it?
- How do they invest?
- Also, how do they think about money? Do they visualise the wealth?
- Is money a concept or a tool for them?

One thing that was clear to me is that wealthy people always:
- Think differently
- Act judiciously
- Spend wisely

They are always well disciplined in their daily lives, which means the creation of wealth is more of a psychology than a science. It is more belief-oriented.

Based on this idea, I gathered inputs and tried to divide wealth creation concepts into five parts:
- Thinking about wealth
- Becoming wealthy
- Cultivating a wealthy mindset
- Keeping and staying wealthy, and
- Sharing

These five parts are self-explanatory and easy to understand, but difficult to practice. If implemented correctly, then it will certainly help to create and maintain wealth.

I use the word 'doctrine' instead of principles because these sets of things are based on beliefs, much like a doctrine. Beliefs are the most important thing for achieving the desired results, so all the sets of principles are stated here as the doctrine.

I would also like to mention here the usage of various mythological, religious, and psychological concepts on money for my practical research on becoming wealthy, along with Sufi, Japanese, Chinese, and Hindu beliefs on money.

So here I am sharing it all in this book with an aim to help you achieve your goals. Enjoy the ride towards making yourself, and your family, wealthy.

My best wishes,
Mithun Desai

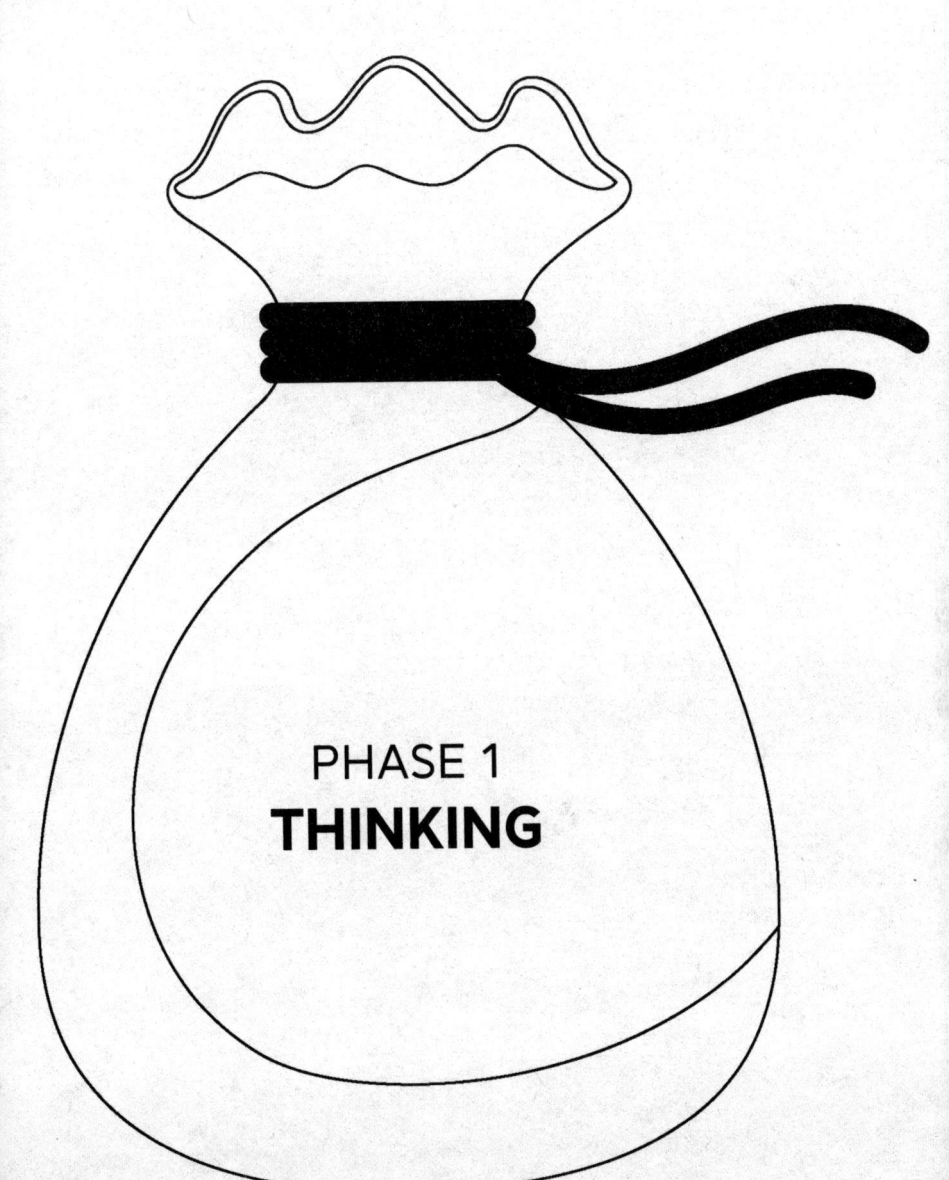

Doctrine 1

Understanding Money

MONEY PLAYS A vital role in our life. We need money for almost everything—it can work for you if you assign it a clear goal. But, money will sit idle if you simply hoard it. Money has no form—it is beyond currency notes or coins; it is a concept.

Money is a mind game associated with the owner's thinking and manifestations. If you try looking up on Google 'what is money?', you will get an answer similar to this: 'Money is a commodity generally accepted as a medium of economic exchange.' If money is a medium then its form can change as per time and requirement. Studying the evolution of money will give a better understanding of this.

What is wealth? Google says—Money is a medium of exchange that represents value and is used to pay for goods and services and repay loans. Wealth is the value of a person's, community's or country's assets, minus their debts. So, you have to understand the concept of money and wealth before walking on the path of wealth creation. Money is intangible and is without form and shape. It is a concept, a belief, and so you have to be very clear about it. You have to understand fear, greed, gratification, risk, power of compounding, and asset allocation among other things to build a wealth. The power of visualisation and the discipline of setting a goal is equally important.

This book will unfold the magic of money and the step-by-step process of wealth creation. Though all these doctrines outlined here are simple to understand, they are difficult to practice. So with this brief note, let's start our journey to create wealth.

Doctrine 2

Set Your Goals And Objectives

HAVING UNDERSTOOD THE concept of wealth and its significance, it's time to set your goals based on your future requirements. This means setting your destination and a timeline to reach there. Just as you schedule your daily tasks, you have to plan your end goals and chalk out a schedule to reach them.

The following pointers will help you determine your goals easily:

- Your goals have to be SMART:
  S–Simple and Specific
  M–Measurable
  A–Achievable
  R–Realistic and Relevant
  T–Time Bound.
- Your goals need to be specific, clear, and simple to understand, leaving no room for any ambiguity.
- You should be able to measure your goals from time to

time and monitor your step-by-step journey towards your goals.
- Your environment, profession, skills, risk profile, and location determine your success. Your goals should be in sync with all these factors so that they can be achieved easily.
- You should research well before determining your goals and gain insight into your sector and its economic and political relevance.
- Another fundamental thing is the time frame to achieve your goals. While deciding the time frame, you should consider your age, the current rate of inflation, and the overall growth rate year to year registered in your segment. Some industries allow overnight success, although they come with high risk.
- In the end, don't broadcast your goals to the public or anybody because people and their opinions might discourage you from achieving your goals.

In a nutshell, keep your goals with you all the time, look at them several times a day, and keep a close track on your journey.

Doctrine 3

Work Hard To Achieve Your Goals

NOW THAT YOU have clearly defined your goals, you need to work endlessly and passionately to achieve them. The differentiating factor is the passion that drives you towards your goal. Without passion, you cannot work endlessly. It will be reduced to a cumbersome and laborious chore and not a goal. To achieve your goals you have to work 24x7.

It is not physical work that we are talking about. It is the combination of systematic work coupled with visualisation, passion, confidence, and belief. Remember, becoming wealthy is not about inheritances or overnight miracles. You need to practically utilise your potential to the maximum to achieve your goal of becoming rich.

There will be obstacles in your path, but if you have a passion and fire for it then it will be a joyful ride. Money is not earned by chance, it is hard-earned with focus, passion, and systematic work.

Look at the wealthy people around you. Dhirubhai Ambani, Azim Premji, Bill Gates, Steve Jobs—the list is endless. All of them had a passion and a burning desire to create wealth, for which they worked relentlessly.

It is not that only industrialists make money. Many artists, musicians, and sports professionals have created wealth with their acumen and professional skills. Let me tell you about one of my clients who has created wealth from scratch. He had no educational background, and no support. All he had was the desire to become rich which made him a good observer and helped him identify many opportunities. He started trading cosmetic items bought at cheaper rates and selling at premium prices in some identified markets. Observing the demand and the gaps in the market, he created an FMCG brand which nobody had ever thought of. In his journey, many people discouraged him, but he was clear about his goal and belief which turned his venture into a multi-million empire. He used to say that if you have faith in yourself and your goal and work hard with a focused aim, then money will follow you automatically.

There is no shortcut to creating wealth; the way may be long with lots of hurdles but with a clear goal and consistency, you can achieve your goal. If you are ready to be hard-working, dedicated, focused, ambitious, and sacrificing, then nobody can stop you from becoming wealthy. You have to learn from your mistakes, or better still, learn and earn from mistakes. Have an eye for detail, ask questions, value people, products, and money, but above all, stay focused. And you will see miraculous results. Another one of my clients always told me—work hard and good things will happen. Make every obstacle an opportunity.

To give you another nugget of wisdom from one of my clients: the size of the door of success is always very narrow, but the atrium is always very big. You have to keep trying and put effort into entering through the door of success. Have patience because once you enter that door then there is a huge space for everything; there are many rooms, pathways, and many other entries. The challenge is to get your foot in the door.

So, be ready for the journey of creating wealth with one mantra—there is no place for lazy people on this journey.

Doctrine 4

Cultivate Strong Money Beliefs

WE ALL HAVE our personal beliefs in money depending on our religion, social environment, upbringing, and geographical locations. While most beliefs can be baseless and biased, without any relevant logic, it must be accepted that money is a consequence and not a reward. It depends on your money beliefs and the hard work you do to earn it. Most religions teach us that money is the root of all bad things, and hence one should not have it in excess. The greedy always seek money and do all the wrong deeds to acquire it, but this is not always true.

While many may adopt wrong measures to get money, here, we will learn to get money with our skills, knowledge, and systematic planning. Here, we decide what money means to us, why we want it, how we plan to use it, how we want to preserve it to build wealth eventually with our planning, and how to share it.

Many believe one has to work too hard to be wealthy and sacrifice a lot, forgetting one's family, hobbies, and recreation. But, no, it is not true. The journey of wealth is always exciting and fulfilling. Observe the wealthy people and their lifestyle, how they enjoy their life, and how they enjoy the company of their family and friends. Money is meant to fulfil all your desires and to enjoy what you like.

A very wealthy of my clients once told me that he follows the principle that, 'Work in a way that any hard worker will be amazed, and live in a way that any king will envy you.' It means life is to enjoy and do whatever you like, and you need money for that. Determining how much money you need to enjoy your life is crucial to goal planning.

Some people also believe that once you become wealthy, you are alone; people start to envy you and, ultimately, hate you and keep away. However, even this is not true. The rich are always famous, and people seek their company; they want to be with rich people. Neither is it true that money can be earned by only wrong means, greed and dishonesty. Get rid of any such beliefs. You need to understand that the desire to earn money is inherently good. Wanting more money is not bad, provided it is hard-earned. Money can be earned with knowledge and expertise.

To earn money, you have to prepare yourself first. So, first, check your money beliefs, and write down how you visualise money; do this exercise in a quiet environment for at least a week. Fix a particular time to write down your money beliefs. After a week, check your money beliefs and get rid of stigmas and myths, if any. Strengthen your belief that money is essentially good and it is the only thing which can make you and your family happy. Discuss your money beliefs with your friends and family, and educate them about the accurate meaning of money because they are your companions during your money journey. All wealthy people are very clear about their money beliefs and don't harbour any doubts or myths regarding that. They are clear about their wealth—they want more wealth, they want to preserve and increase their wealth, they use wealth to reach their goals and purpose and they even want to share their wealth for the right cause.

If you work hard to earn money, there are more chances that you will acquire it. Remember, you are getting money as compensation for your expertise, astute beliefs and hard work. The harder and smarter you work, the more chances to earn better. Wealth is your friend and not a foe; it is a necessity. If we need money for every requirement in our life, then how can it be bad? It is not, and you should be very clear about it.

So, to begin with, start noting down your money beliefs and be clear that money is good, and it is good to have more money.

Doctrine 5

Observe The Wealthy Around You

TO LEARN HOW to earn more money, you should start observing the wealthy people around you. Understand why they wanted all the money they made in the first place, how they spend their money, what is the purpose which drives them to earn more and more money, and why and how money-making becomes a hobby for some. It is noteworthy that the wealth the rich have accumulated is not for spending only on them; everyone has some purpose to earn more money. Why do you think Warren Buffett wants to earn more money? He is living an austere life—driving an age-old car, living in a simple home, and having a humble office with the bare minimum employees already with him for years. Despite being a major shareholder in Boeing, he doesn't have an aircraft of his own. He has donated half of his wealth to a charity. Notwithstanding this, earning money through hard work is his habit and hobby.

Learn from the wealthy that making money is their passion, habit, and hobby. I have observed many wealthy people working endlessly to earn money while living a minimalistic life. Those who want to spend money to show off are the ones who adopt the wrong means to earn, while those with a clear purpose to earn have a passion for earning money. One of my clients struggled to create wealth—a struggle that few can survive. At one point in time, out of his desperation to earn, he would tell his wife that if he failed to earn the required amount, he would rob a bank. It does not mean that he wants to rob a bank and make easy money; rather, it denotes his strong urge to work hard and create wealth. It is such people, driven by a burning desire, who can make money. After a point, it is irrelevant how much money you have over your basic needs; it is relevant only as long as you have a clear purpose for earning money. Also, your purpose keeps changing—you reach one peak and aim for the next.

All rich people have a dream and want money to fulfil it; once their dream is fulfilled, they see another to keep themselves constructively busy. Why did Walt Disney want to make more money? And what did he do with all the money he earned? What has Rockefeller done with whatever he has earned? Money will flow only when you have a clear purpose. The Universe believes in abundance, and there is no limit on how much money you can earn because the Universe doesn't believe in boundaries. However, if you want to earn money only to buy luxury cars, have a lavish lifestyle, or build grand properties like farmhouses, or lake houses, then you should aim for clarity too. What is your perceived limit of spending on such high-maintenance things? What is your purpose behind possessing all those things? One of my wealthy acquaintances shared with me that all the luxury brands make him insecure which then led him to realise that the true utilisation of money is not in buying luxury things. And that's why you need to be clear about why you want to earn more.

The differentiating factor between the wealthy and the not-so-wealthy is their clarity on earning. Be it for your family, luxury, medical needs, child education, or anything else, you should have the clarity that most rich people have. They are also clear about what they don't need more money for. This deserves equal consideration since the need and purpose to earn money varies. So, like most wealthy people, you should also have your set agenda to earn. Rich people also know that money gets money. And that's why eventually the rich get richer. You can also realise during your money-making journey that once you have some money, it can grow exponentially if you work towards your goal with discipline. Moreover, observe how the wealthy refrain from spending all their money; they keep some for multiplying further. You have to invest and reinvest your money wisely for it to multiply. The wise and the wealthy put some money away into breeding so that it multiplies, some for covering expenses, and some for investing in their inherent business or profession. They have clarity of purpose, focused mind, hard yet smart work, and covert goals kept to themselves.

So, have a mindset like the wealthy and keep working towards your goals.

Doctrine 6

Don't Envy

WE ALL ARE different in every possible way—thinking, nature, abilities, passion, hobbies, ambition, and the list continues. We also have different skill sets, visions, and future goals. The only common thing is time; all of us have 24 hours a day, 60 minutes per hour, and 60 seconds in a minute. Within this limited time, how can we earn money doing what we like the most, and what we know is the most important? Money is not earned by a coincidence, it is the result of what you do, how you do it, whether you enjoy doing it and how clear you are about your goal. So if anybody earns more than you, there is no point in envying them as your requirement, goal, and use of money can be entirely different from others.

If you enquire others about their need for money or their goal, then you will get surprising answers. Most people are not clear about this. They need money because others have, and some already have a lot but want to add more to it. Rather than envying others, one should gain clarity about their money requirement and goal.

Money acquired with a goal-centric approach can give your life not only a purpose but all the comforts and luxuries as well. One of my wealthy clients has everything one could dream of. Yet he is always dissatisfied and complaining, always finding reasons to be unhappy. There is no rhyme or reason in envying such a person. Money is good when you have a clear understanding of using it. The journey of getting money becomes exciting and challenging with a clear purpose and goal. Rather than envying rich people, one should learn from them. Figure out how he earned money, what was his goal, passion, and skill. How methodical he is in his approach and more. One thing is clear—only those people have legit money who have worked hard, have a goal-oriented mindset, are passion driven, and love what they do. If you are earning money doing work you don't like, then the possibilities of getting wealth out of your activities will be minimised. That's why envying the rich and blindly copying them or their approach will not help as his likings and yours might be different.

Envying the rich is a very common human tendency. Instead, studying the rich can be a strong motivating factor that can guide you on your money-making journey. Turn your envy into planning your financial goals by observing the rich. It can help you gain insight into your money-making journey. Acknowledging and regulating envy is equally important. If not checked, envy can harm your mental balance and affect your overall well-being. The best way is to use envy as a motivator. As discussed earlier, rich people are not always necessarily happy, as happiness comes from real contentment and that can come by the purpose and achievement of your goals. There are different sources of satisfaction and happiness, money is one of them but not the only. And that's why goal setting is very important. Goal setting can help you to earn money and once earned, the money can be utilised towards those goals hence it is satisfying. The best way is to have a money mentor, find someone who has earned a lot of money legally, who is spending it wisely, enjoying it and happily living. You can learn a lot from such a mentor.

Successful and rich people have lots of things that can be learned and implemented and that is the core of the *Money Management Doctrine*. When you find a mentor follow his journey closely and implement each learning. *Money Management Doctrine* is also your mentor and it is your interest to follow each doctrine to understand money. You can envy those rich who have got money from the lottery or inheritance, but those people lose money.

Remember, don't envy rich people and upset your mental health. Learn from them as many of them have an inspirational story that can teach many valuable lessons. If possible make them your mentor.

Doctrine 7

If Others Can, So Can You

IF YOU NOTICE, most rich people are either college dropouts or haven't pursued higher studies. Most of them come from humble backgrounds and have many hindrances keeping them from becoming a millionaire or billionaire.

So how did they become so rich? If you take a deeper dive, you will find that the only common factor is their passion to pursue their dreams and goals and crystal-clear vision of what they want and how they want it. Acquiring skills in any field is indispensable for earning well. Even if you have multiple skill sets, focus on the strongest one that you possess. There are other qualities too—vision, clarity of goals, discipline, networking and more—that are important, though not imperative, except one—the fire within to earn money. As has been understood, having a clear belief in money is half the battle won. Next, your purpose as to why you need money will help you assign your goals. With role clarity, your way forward gets smooth.

Later, qualities like passion and discipline will help you work towards achieving your goals. Becoming rich is not a goal to be achieved overnight, but multiple goals will take you there collectively. Persistence can also help you achieve your goals. It is the never-say-die attitude that helps the rich as they are never afraid to lose and always welcome failures as their learning opportunities. All these virtues and attributes can be found commonly. Education, talent, family background, geographical location, opportunities—nothing is more important than having clarity about why you need money and your willingness to follow your journey with full passion and vigour.

There are many stories of rags to riches that give one insight that anybody can make money. We can name rich people from different fields who have acclaimed their fortune fighting against all the odds. So one thing should be clear in your mind—you can be rich, no matter your age, location, or adversities. As per *Forbes*, almost two-thirds of the world's 946 billionaires have made their fortune from scratch, relying on sheer grit and determination, and not good genes. All these diverse stories of billionaires give us the motivation that anybody can make money. You are no less.

Remember, what matters the most is earning money with all the legal means. Your earnings should not harm others. Check your means of earning money and be conscious about your ways. You should enjoy your money-making journey, and you can do that by earning it the right way. A blissful life with lots of money and peaceful sleep at night can only be earned legally and ethically.

Doctrine 8

Wealth Is A Consequence, Not A Reward

WEALTH IS A CONSEQUENCE, not a reward. It is not about your talent, smartness, or education, nor does it matter whether you deserve it. Money can be made with the right efforts and not by virtue. If you work hard to earn money, your chances of earning well will be brighter. Money is the compensation given to you for solving a problem. The bigger the problem you solve, the better you earn. So, to make more money, try and think about solving many people's problems collectively rather than focusing on one or two people's problem.

Money is a payment you earn for your hard work, acumen, and skills. It means the harder and smarter you work, the more you earn. Let's understand this by solving a problem. Every human being has different needs. Somebody is hungry and looking for food to satisfy his hunger. So, if you have a food joint, you are solving people's problem of hunger pangs and getting your money by solving that particular problem. Now, how many people's hunger can your food joint solve every day? Is it 100 or 1000? You will be getting money as payment for the food you serve them. If you have 10 food joints, you are solving 1000 to 10,000 people's hunger problem. So think in terms of numbers. Likewise, McDonald's is earning heaps of money from its food as it has over lacs of outlets worldwide, catering to the hunger of crores. The logic here is simple, there are many problems you can solve encompassing categories like food, finance, entertainment, education, social, the list is endless. Choose your strength and identify the core problem, focus specifically on it and solve it, try to reach as many people as possible facing this core problem, offer them a solution, and get your payment. In this digital world, reaching the target audience is easy.

So if you can explore the digital medium to solve people's problems, your chances of getting more money will increase. Observe how marketplace brands are solving people's problems digitally and getting money. This simple formula is derived from the complex economic principle of Double Coincidence of Wants.

Money solves the problem of double coincidence of wants by acting as a medium of exchange. It implies a situation where two parties agree to sell and buy each other's commodities/services, that is, what one party desires to sell is exactly what the other party wishes to buy. Money does away with this tedious and complex situation by acting as a medium of exchange that can be used for each commodity/service. For example, if an ice cream vendor wants a bicycle but the bicycle manufacturer wants clothes, and not ice cream, the vendor can use the money to obtain a bicycle. He does need to adhere to the bicycle man's needs though because money acts as the common medium of exchange. Similarly, the bicycle manufacturer can then use the money to buy clothes.

Earning money is nothing but getting your payment for solving people's problems and that's why it is not a coincidence but a consequence—the payment and not the reward. The word 'consequence' here means the consequence of a business idea, acumen, skill, effort, and hard work. This consequence is being paid as a payment and is not a reward.

So, to earn money find your core competence, niche, macro-niche and micro-niche, and structure a strategy around it to make a product or service which you can use to solve people's problems and earn money.

Doctrine 9

Money Gets Money

MONEY ATTRACTS MONEY. It is a universal truth. The rich always get richer. You feel sad when you look around and find people struggling to get their necessities and living a deprived life. Because they don't have money, they can't change their life. That's why we should understand the importance of money and have a clear belief in money.

Money tends to grow, and it is a truth that rich people know well, hence they put their money where it will grow. Rich people have a multidimensional approach to increasing their wealth—once they get a good amount of money, they focus on preserving it and making more money out of it. When you observe the rich around you, you will find their diverse outlook towards their investment and focused financial goals for the future.

Many rich people have money from multiple sources like salaries, dividend income, rental income, real estate, mutual fund investments, and gold among others. With a diverse investment in many assets, they get the advantage of diversification of risk; if one category slows down, the other might keep growing. This passive income is crucial as it keeps growing by compounding effect in less time. Money brings power, and once you get it, you want more. That's why a clear belief in money and a predetermined goal will get you more creative ideas to accumulate wealth. And when you put your money in the correct place, the compounding effects start working, bringing you more money. The term 'rich get richer' is derived from the book *Capital in the Twenty-First Century*, where the author has studied the data of several hundred years supporting the central thesis that the owners of capital accumulate wealth quicker than those who provide labour.

Once you get the money, you will be surprised to see how fast it can grow due to the compounding effects. Whatever you earn, put some in a planned investment where the compound works better. As discussed, the rich are expert in putting their money into diverse assets that get their money growing exponentially. Some rich people hire an expert financial advisor who helps them with the right investment and asset allocation. If you spend all you get, then this doctrine will not work. You must have read about prize-money winners spending all their fortune and not investing wisely, thereby losing an opportunity to grow their money.

Investing is an interesting tool to multiply your money, but even for the investment you need money, so you have to earn using your micro-niche and invest 20 per cent of it. You can soon see your money compounding. When we save and invest money judiciously, money grows exponentially over time due to compounding, as the returns generated on the initial amount begin to earn returns themselves. Due to this snowball effect, even modest investments turn into substantial wealth. We need to have two essential qualities—patience and discipline for compounding to work and do its magic. Very few can harness the power of compounding as they fail to exercise patience and discipline due to fear or greed. Also, the power of compounding can work against us if we borrow money to fund our lifestyle expenses or spend on liabilities disguised as assets.

One of our money beliefs is about the definition of asset and liability. Asset is what we own, and liability is what we owe. This belief has resulted in a false illusion of wealth, and majority kept spending on liabilities disguised as assets, thereby getting stuck in the rat race of earning more and more money due to increasing expenses and EMI. One needs to let go of orthodox money beliefs about assets and liabilities. An asset is anything that increases our income, and liability is what incurs additional expenses. Asset adds to our earnings, and liability adds to our expenses. If we borrow money to fund our lifestyle expenses, the interest on the borrowed amount compounds, leading to a growing debt burden which can go out of control.

It is crucial to understand and harness the power of compounding, whether we are building wealth or managing debt. Remember to put your money in a place from where it can grow. Work on your money beliefs, manage your money well, and let the power of compounding work its magic.

Doctrine 10

Money Is Not A Solution

MONEY IS EVERYTHING, this is the common belief, but, remember, money alone cannot do anything. Money is a currency; it facilitates transactions, but is not a solution to your problems. For example, in case of a disease, money can only buy the best medical help, but it does not guarantee a cure or protect you from disease. Rich people are as prone to disease as poor people. Similarly, money cannot guarantee peace of mind, sound sleep, or even happiness. If we think that we can live a happy life with a lot of money, we are living in an illusion. Money is nothing but a lubricant that smoothens life; it cannot be an engine to propel our life ahead. Though money is essential, it is not a solution for the life problems. It is like finding a cure and then funding that cure with money. Problems like personal, social, and political cannot be solved by money alone.

Wealth and power are the two most powerful symbols of happiness. Money is a symbolic goal that relates to happiness.

But real happiness can be derived by pursuing purpose and meaning. The real purpose of money is to get you financial freedom. If you want to have a life of FFL (Financial Freedom Lifestyle), then the money is indeed important. How? Money can take care of all your financial requirements—living expenses, hobbies, lifestyle expenses, and all your other basic requirements.

With an FFL life you can do things which you like the most and thereby gain happiness and creative satisfaction. So, this is the role of money as seen from a larger perspective. One golden rule worth noting is that money can't buy happiness, but it can give the time and freedom to pursue it. Money provides us with two essential things—time and freedom. When you understand this golden rule, you can peacefully sleep at night, enjoy your money, and take delight in whatever you do.

Money is available freely because our universe believes in abundance. Money is available to all of us and that's what the previous doctrine mentioned—anybody can make money. Many people have made money despite all the adverse conditions and limitations. Dearth of money makes us miserable, so does excess of money as we fail to understand the meaning and purpose of our wealth. Money doesn't buy happiness; all it does is give financial freedom that kick starts our journey towards happiness.

Another money belief to be changed is that financial independence and financial freedom are the same. When we start earning money, we are financially independent as our choice about spending is not dependent on others that is we do not need to ask for money to spend. However, financial freedom is not just about our earning capability. Financial freedom means an abundance of time and money. It is achieved when income is not solely dependent on you. We earn by selling our time and such income is defined as active income. Income that does not require our active involvement is called passive income such as interest, rent, dividend, gain and royalty. Financial freedom is when we enter and exit the economy at our free will. An excess of passive income over active income gives you the luxury to buy time rather than sell it. For wealthy people time is money and their unit of measurement concerning any financial decision (be it earning or spending) is the time component and not money.

It is worth remembering that money is not the end; it is one of the means that can lead to your end goal of living a happy and fulfilling life.

Doctrine 11

Money, Happiness, Price, And Value

THE AGE-OLD question of whether money can buy happiness has always intrigued researchers and the general public. Recent studies have provided compelling evidence that money does play a significant role in enhancing happiness. This chapter delves into the nuances of this relationship, focusing on two distinct types of well-being: experienced well-being, and evaluative well-being.

Experienced well-being refers to the day-to-day feelings and moods that individuals experience. It encompasses the emotional aspects of well-being, such as joy, stress, sadness, and affection. Research indicates that higher income levels are associated with better experienced well-being. People with higher incomes tend to report more positive emotions and fewer negative emotions in their daily lives. That is, higher income levels are linked to better daily emotions, with people generally feeling happier, less stressed, and more content.

Evaluative well-being, on the other hand, involves a

person's overall assessment of their life. It includes how satisfied they are with their life as a whole. Higher income levels are also linked to better evaluative well-being. People with higher incomes often feel more satisfied with their lives and perceive their life circumstances more positively.

Interestingly, the research indicates no specific income threshold where the benefits of higher income plateau. Both experienced and evaluative well-being continue to increase with income, even at higher levels. Higher income continuously enhances happiness, with no apparent limit to its positive impact.

Understanding the relationship between money and happiness has practical implications for individuals and policymakers. For individuals, it highlights the impact of financial stability and growth on enhancing overall well-being. For policymakers, it highlights the importance of creating economic policies that promote income growth and reduce income inequality to add to the well-being of the masses.

It is noteworthy that financial well-being is certainly a crucial component of overall happiness. Why can money deliver happiness and how? It is mainly because of the following reasons:

- Money induced comfort.
- Power and control over things. One of the major reasons for happiness is money giving you an upper hand to control many situations.

However, one thing is fundamentally correct—without a purposeful meaning of money, the accumulation of wealth cannot make you happy.

Happiness is a state of mind. So, when you have enough money to pay your bills, you can achieve this state of mind which, if combined with the overall purpose of getting more money, makes you happy from inside and that is what real happiness is.

Doctrine 12

Money And Mind

MONEY AND MIND have a unique connection. Should we have money on mind, or mind on money? Money has a strong influence—on our life, thinking and perception. Money related thinking is primarily driven by emotion and impulse, and less by logic and reason. When we think of money, we are not just thinking about money. Our decision about money, spending, investment, etc. is based on our belief, bias, impulse, and financial habits. Many of us are victims of impulsive spending or overlooking investment. Understanding the difference between saving and investment also depends on our grooming and surroundings. As far as money is concerned, we are not very open to discussions; we don't like to discuss salaries, remunerations, and investments. Financial decisions are crucial for creating wealth and require metaheuristics to quickly process the financial information.

How you react and act in different financial situations is also based on the wiring of your mind based on your financial habits.

The mind is multifaceted and it behaves in a complex manner as far as the financial decisions are concerned. It is hard to give a one-size-fits-all financial advice. It is necessary to develop the skills to understand our preferences, goals, risk appetite, and our money beliefs while making any financial decisions. In most of our financial decisions, we make mistakes due to focusing more on the present than the future. It is because the present is more related to immediate gratification while the future is more salient and less concrete. Our financial decisions are not apt because of a lack of financial education and unwillingness to learn and upskill or a combination of both. Similarly, we do not understand interest and inflation in the correct way, the power of compounding, and the difference between saving money and growing money. Saving versus spending, our thoughts on debt, our inability to make quick financial decisions are crucial for our financial planning. We have to learn and understand that emotions affect financial decisions more than anything.

Our money mind denotes our emotional relationship with money. Our biases around money, as discussed in the book, are based on our beliefs, upbringing, and values. Our money mind drives us to earn and save more money. You have to train your mind to make money. Mental imaging techniques and mental rehearsal are powerful psychological ways used by billionaires, entrepreneurs, and athletes to achieve their goals. You must have heard the stories of sportspeople playing their game in mind first and then on the field. Likewise, rehearsing each step of your money-making journey can help you stimulate your mind. With a stimulated mind you can earn better as it gives you more power to achieve your goals.

Sometimes you might wonder how less capable people make more money. The answer is they use these mind techniques of stimulation for making money. Here are some of the steps you can follow too:
- Find a problem to be solved for making money.
- Have clarity in mind that you can make money despite all the hurdles.
- Practice gratitude as it leads to an action.

There are some mental techniques that rich people use to make money. Let's overview some here:
- Rich people tell themselves that there is no shortage of money.
- They consider money-making as a game, making it more fun, and less stressing.
- Rich people set their expectations high.
- Many rich people see money as a friend; they personify it, as if, money is a human.
- They work on their money beliefs.

Money is earned faster and better with a clear mind. There are several techniques available, but all lead to the central point that is—earn with your mind, and not time. The basic thing to learn at this point is that you have to train your mind to make money. You have to recalibrate your brain through integration.

Doctrine 13

It Is Harder To Manage Yourself Than Manage Money

SO FAR WE have studied twelve money management doctrines and learned that it takes discipline, consistency, clear and well-defined goals based on purpose, and a well-trained mind to make money. Do you have all these qualities? Before you answer that you have to consider—do you know yourself? Do you know yourself completely or vaguely? Do you have willpower? Have you ever tested your willpower or mind? Have you set any goals in the past and achieved them? We sometimes test ourselves and our mind and willpower, for example, when we decide to quit smoking or any other bad habit. Similarly, following a strict diet or a workout regimen also tests your willpower.

These help us realise if we are strong-minded, lazy, or impulsive. So you have to know yourself first. Do you have the qualities needed to earn money? Are you determined enough to earn more? Do you have enough stamina and willpower? Are you clear and focused on your future goals? Are you disciplined enough to follow the journey to become rich? After all, do you want to be rich? You have to find an answer to all these.

Remember that making money is a skill learned and acquired only when you are ready for it. You need to analyse yourself thoroughly and find out if you have what it takes to be wealthy. The same applies to any goal that you want to achieve in life. If you want to become a cricketer and play for India, you have to plan it accordingly—start playing from the school level gradually moving to college, district, Ranji Trophy and so on. You have to plan each step diligently and start executing them one after another. If you have ever observed the rich around you, then you must have realised that when they started their money-making journey they had strong willpower and a fire in them to make enormous sacrifices, if the need be. You can earn and manage money if you can manage yourself. So, start managing yourself from now.

The truth is that most of the time we are not equipped with the right skills, mental strength, or willpower which triggers our financial efforts to make more money. Most of the time the problem is not money; it is us, ourselves. We have to start managing ourselves, our behaviour, and mental space in our money-making journey.

Self-management is the personal application of behaviour change tactics that produce a desired change in behaviour[1]. In simpler terms, it means taking control of your actions by

---

1 Cooper, Heron, Heward (2007) *Applied Behaviour Analysis*. Pearson

applying techniques that help you change your behaviour to reach your goals. It could involve setting personal rules, monitoring your progress, and rewarding yourself for bringing positive changes. The idea is that by managing your behaviour, you can improve your habits and achieve better results in various aspects of your life. To understand the concept of managing yourself, let's focus on another famous concept: Pay Yourself First. This concept has a tremendous power for making one financially independent. It was first used in a book called, *The Richest Man In Babylon*. This converted into a very strong personal finance rule by Robert Kiyosaki in his book *Rich Dad Poor Dad*, where he explained that this concept is more self-disciplined. Here are the excerpts from the book:

Pay yourself First: Understand the power of self-discipline. If you cannot control yourself, do not try to get rich. It makes no sense to earn money and blow it away. There is a deep understanding and logic in this concept. We are earning not to spend, but to attain financial freedom. The rule does encourage self-sacrifice or financial abstinence. But it doesn't mean pay yourself first and starve.

Life is meant to be enjoyed; if you call on your financial genius, you can have all the luxuries of life, and get rich and pay bills, without sacrificing the good life. This is financial intelligence. This concept says that whatever you earn first put it into investment and generate passive income. Though it is a good concept, I am seeing it from a different perspective. You pay yourself first by preparing and managing yourself to be ready for FFL so that you can earn, manage, create and share wealth.

Doctrine 14

Money And/Or Passion

BOTH MONEY AND passion are indispensable in life. If you can make money by following your passion, then it is the best thing in life. If you are making money by doing something which you don't like, then after some time your dissatisfaction will suppress you, and you will get frustrated. If you are pursuing your passion but not making money, then have patience, for your passion will get you both money as well as recognition.

The most important thing is to follow your passion. Develop yourself around your passion, master your skills, find your micro-niche, and see money coming to you.

Passion versus money is an age-old dilemma. Many have to do and follow the job which they might not like but have to do as the money is important. Many a times we come across stories of people who wanted to become a cricketer, actor, or singer, but couldn't pursue their passion as they had to take up a job or business to earn money. But here is the catch. If you can earn money and reach financial freedom then you can follow your passion without any obstacles. Moreover, you can also follow your passion while pursuing a job to earn and attain financial freedom.

Don't hold your passion back; passion is an emotion that lives with you throughout your life and can show up anytime. So keep following your passion and try to develop your skills around your passion as it can help in making more money.

Imagine that you are earning good but there is no opportunity, learning, growth and potential that eventually ruins your career.

Learn how you can make money from your passion as it offers the best combination for a happy and satisfactory life even amidst adversities. Let's ponder over words from Steve Jobs on this subject:

> 'Your work is going to fill a large part of life, and the only way to be truly satisfied is to do what you believe is great work. And the only way to do great work is to love what you do.'

Most often we believe that passion is a hobby which can't fetch money. For example, somebody who likes cooking might feel that it is a hobby with no monetary benefit. Similarly, one may like yoga but not be able to see it as a profession. This is where Steve Jobs's view comes into play. He believed that a passion with a purpose can change the world. And the real challenge is to turn your passion into purpose.

Passion is more of a fun activity with fulfilment, while purpose is all about making an impact. One should aim at striking a balance between passion and purpose to derive money as well as satisfaction.

We have discussed about finding a micro-niche and purpose that can be converted into a profession to bring money as well as happiness. For example, if your passion is yoga, you can find your purpose in teaching yoga to millions of people, making them yoga gurus to change the world by bringing health and happiness. With this end in view, you can work around this purpose, build your digital course and earn both money and fame.

If you are more passionate about what you do, then you will be more inclined towards working hard and upskilling in your niche, to increase your earnings and chances of success.

With passion and enthusiasm combined, one becomes more resilient and ready to face struggle better than anybody else. If you follow your passion there is a higher chance that money and success will follow because the time and effort invested in your work come with enthusiasm and zeal.

To earn money from your passion you need to consider some simple things:
- Find a micro-niche in your passion and make it your profession.
- Consider building up a course around your passion and micro-niche that can be sold digitally.
- Talk about your passion so that people know about it. Create a brand around your passion through social media and various digital platforms.
- If needed, provide free service, coaching around your passion/ micro-niche so that people start knowing about your offerings.

- Set goals to earn desired amount from your passion and start working towards it.

And the last one insight:

Understand that your passion is a product/service that can be bought by many if converted into a brand and marketed properly. Find out about your passion and know which industry it represents. In most cases, it is entertainment and education. Converting your passion into a business was a challenge earlier, but now everything has changed with technological advancement. You can easily build up your brand around your passion and design your course to sell it through the internet on various platforms.

So, start working around your passion and build a brand around your micro-niche. Follow your passion, and money will follow you.

Doctrine 15

We Are Here To Make Money

THE SOLE PURPOSE of mankind is to live happily, have a family, and succeed in life. We have religion, community, theories about the universe, mankind, and a purpose in life. So, why are we here and what is the purpose of life?

Humans have their needs and aspirations. Progressing in life, we humans establish various belief systems. We form our beliefs surrounding money and which might be the main obstacle in getting money.

When we look around, we see many people are without money or less money and they are struggling throughout their life for money. Despite acumen, intelligence, and skills, many struggle for money. On the other hand, there are people who have all the money they need or even more, without any education background, skills, or intelligence. There is no correlation as you can get all types of stories around money.

One common thing which I came across throughout my professional career as a financial advisor is that money is a mind thing more than anything else.

We are here to make money and money is not evil at all. We all have our dreams, longings, cravings, duties, and goals, and to support all these things we need money.

Money is centered on our needs and longings and we need it for the betterment of our and our family's life. We all want to be rich, spend money on things, give back to society, and do some meaningful things for our family and planet Earth, and we need money for all this.

Like it or not, but money is everything and once we get a lot of it, it is nothing. When you have a lot of money then you tend to spend it more for others than for yourself. Money is power; it gives you safety. Money gives you security, freedom, and power to pursue what you like, and these things lead to happiness.

Money gives you a better life to live; something that all of us need. Money allows people the autonomy to make choices about how they live their lives. As discussed earlier, people's emotional well-being improves with wealth. Of course, there are other factors contributing to happiness in life, but money is the most important among those.

When your money belief is well-tuned, when you are earning money legally by following your passion, then money is a blessing.

So, remember one basic point:

We are here to make money by doing things that we like. The money we earn should be legal money so that we can add to the happiness of not only our family, but our society, nation and planet as well.

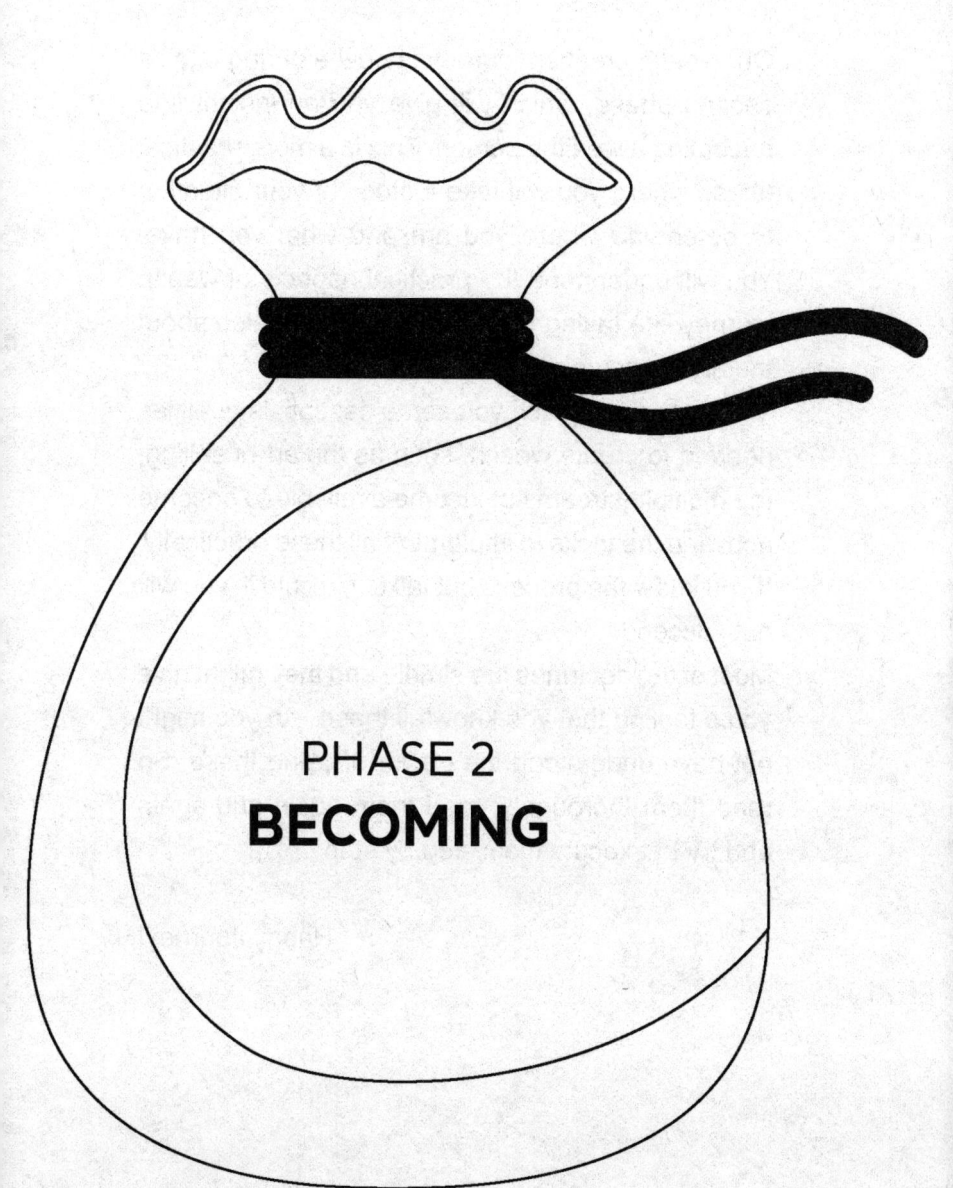

PHASE 2
BECOMING

Our wealth creation journey is now entering into its second phase, which will give you an insight into becoming a wealthy person. This is a more practical phase where you will take a stock of your situation to determine where you are and what you have. You will understand the practical aspects of wealth journey like taking risk, speculation and also about the art of accumulation.

This phase will teach you some essentials qualities needed to create wealth, such as the art of selling, the multiple streams of income available to become rich, and the tricks to implement all these practically. If you know the process but fail to execute it, you will not succeed.

Most of the doctrines are simple and they might give you a feeling that you know all these, yet you might not have understood the power of using these. So read them thoroughly; read them again and again and try to execute them step by step.

Happy Journey!

Doctrine 16

Chalk Out A Plan

WORK ON A plan before moving further. You should know where you are standing now. In any journey, your movement mapping can guide you to plan further trips. You have to do a financial audit on yourself and your family. Collect all the relevant information, like your bank balance, investments in various assets, loans, insurance, health insurance, credit card payments, etc. Make a checklist to get all the information that may include loans, credit score, savings, investments, property list, assets, cars, jewellery and so on.

Make a balance sheet and check the fund flow to take stock of the situation. Accordingly, prepare a future requirement list which might include expenses like children's education, vacations, daily expenses, contingency fund, etc. Make a list of fixed and variable expenses. From this plan, prepare a fund requirement list for the next 5, 10, and 25 years. Now review it. Discuss with your family and seek their feedback/suggestions. Try to focus and get clarity on your fund requirements for the future. Calculate your income as earned from the different sources—passive, active, or through investments. Also, keep provision for unforeseen expenses to have complete clarity about your financial status.

Now, based on your financial status make a plan which will give you an idea about how you can meet your future expenses, how much funding you need for your future, and what resources you have for it. This will give you a good plan of action, indicating what you should do and what not. The plan will put into your perspective the past, present, and future finances. It will guide you better to form a strategy to get the required money.

The financial audit will help you know and understand where you are now and where you want to reach. It will be the blueprint of how you will reach there and by when? The plan will give you many insights. For example, if you have a job with a salary that is decent but not enough to fulfil your financial goals, then your plan will indicate that. Based on that indication, your mind will start exploring ways to get extra income. You might also think of switching over your job or looking for an alternative to your job. Your plan should include all the possibilities like changing career, starting a new venture, sourcing multiple incomes, making investments, working on your niche and micro-niche and finding out how to generate income, paying back all your loans/mortgages, and so on. Wealth can be created by selling products and services and not by merely earning a salary.

'Good fortune is what happens when opportunity meets with planning.'—Thomas Edison.

Planning is everything. We will learn many other doctrines to help you to plan your financial journey. You have to only stick to your planning and goals to get your desired wealth.

Here is one simple checklist as a reference for your personal financial audit:
- Review your account balances.
- Review your debt.
- Know your credit history.
- Write down your expected future income.
- Review your savings.
- Review your investments.
- Review your real estate.
- List down your future expenses.
- Make your contingency expense plan.
- Create a financial plan keeping in mind all the above points.

So, let's start the planning, because a good plan today is better than a perfect plan tomorrow. When you have a concrete plan, your mind comes up with ways to execute it.

Doctrine 17

Have A Good Grip Over Your Finance

ONE OF MY clients always used to say that if you want to create wealth, stop the leakage. Similarly, my grandfather used to scold my grandmother for wasting water. He used to say that if you run water freely and not repair water leakage, you will run out of water and with that your money, too. The context here is that a small leakage leads to a bigger one and everything that you have can be drained out fast, whether it is money or water. Interest, taxation, uninvested money, unplanned expenses, impulsive and wrong buying of things—these are some examples of money leakage.

To control your finances you have to first stop the money leakages. Unplanned expenses with credit cards is the biggest leakage of your money as you tend to spend due to immediate gratification syndrome. If you want to stop this leakage then cancel all your credit cards with immediate effect. However, you can keep one card and try to avoid keeping multiple of them. Also, keep a check on every expense. Track the interest you are paying for your loans, credit cards, etc. Check if you are paying unnecessarily high interest. If possible, don't take loans at all. If you develop a habit of keeping all records of your expenses, including interest money, you will be able to identify your leakages to rectify them. Before taking a loan or insurance, conduct a thorough research and negotiate for a better deal. This will prevent a big leakage. Also, keep an eye on hidden expenses, like unnecessary subscriptions, and some unnoticed direct debits. Keep a tab on the premiums for all types of insurances—accident, life, health, etc. Curb your impulsive online shopping sprees. Keep an auto debit mandate for premiums and utility bills. This will ensure that the payment deadline is not missed and you do not have to pay the penalties. Planning and maintaining an emergency budget for illnesses, accidents, or unforeseen expenses will also save you from huge money leakages. One last thing, observe rich people around you; they are expert in avoiding leakages. Sharing two more golden rules to control your finances:

- **Delay the gratification:** Resist the temptation of an immediate reward in favour of a future reward. You can invest your money instead of spending on an immediate reward which can be extended for the future. Although this is difficult to practice, you can master it to save money and invest it in your goals to achieve financial independence. Research[2] has proved that those who have practiced delayed gratification have been able to create wealth.

---

2 Wikipedia *Stanford Marshmallow Experiment* [Online] Retrieved from: https://en.wikipedia.org/wiki/Stanford_marshmallow_experiment

Delayed Gratification was first tested in the famous 1970 Stanford marshmallow experiment by psychologist Walter Mitchel and his team. They tested self-control on young children for not eating marshmallows. The results show that the kids who mastered delayed gratification had better overall life outcomes. One important thing is you don't have to delay gratification all the time, if we do that then we will miss all the fun of life. You have to see the difference between immediate and delayed rewards and before deciding on this.

- **Have a spending fast (Fasting):** You can observe a spending fast where you spend minimally or only on those things which are essential. Spend nothing for a while, and choose between spending sprees and wealth. Take a prosperity route and postpone the spending. Think that you can always buy better things in future. Live a minimalist life, and understand the difference between need and want. If you follow this for some time then it can change your habit and outlook on money.

To conclude, a strong hold on finances indicates your knowledge about your money—where is your money coming from and going to. Eliminate all the unnecessary expenses and check for leakages to ensure better money management.

Doctrine 18

Look Wealthy, Act Wealthy, And Become Wealthy

HAVE YOU EVER noticed that by looking confident, powerful, and smart, you can attract a lot of attention? What will happen if you step into any hotel or restaurant and look and act wealthy? Yes, you will get the best attention and services. Your behaviour can make you look rich.

Lifestyle changes can also trigger your urge to become rich. Show up and never show off. Act confident and elegant. The mindset which separates the middle class from the millionaire class can be developed by looking, behaving, and thinking like a wealthy person. Your earning potential will depend on your mindset. By looking, powerful and confident, you can win many battles.

You have to focus on self-grooming to make you look rich. It requires a lot of effort, and remember only the right efforts can get you the right results. It is said that you have to dress up for success. Recent studies[3] proved that wearing good outfits can influence how people perceive you; it gives you confidence and can even affect your income. People judge you from your appearance. A study conducted by Columbia Business School[4] proved that a well-dressed person feels more confident, powerful, and focused on details. People always look up to stylish people and perceive them as leaders. There are many research studies on this subject to help you understand and believe that spending on proper clothing is worth it. When you dress well you are showing your self-respect. Good clothing reflects your reliability, trustworthiness, and success. Your outfits speak a lot about yourself and it helps to create a lasting impression. Have you ever felt confident and powerful on wearing fresh, new clothes? That's because good attire creates confidence within you. It works at the psychological level. Ever noticed that whenever you have new gym wear, you like to go to the gym, or if you have new running shoes you prefer to go jogging? It is a placebo effect, how you look on the

---

3   National Library of Medicine *Dress is a Fundamental Component of Person Perception* [Online] Retrieved from: https://www.ncbi.nlm.nih.gov/pmc/articles/PMC10559650/ Association for Psychological Science *When Clothing Style Influences Cognitive Style* [Online] Retrieved from: https://www.psychologicalscience.org/news/minds-business/when-clothing-style-influences-cognitive-style.html#.WTmBucaZNBw

4   Columbia Business School *The Symbolism of Workplace Attire* [Online] Retrieved from: https://business.columbia.edu/cgi-leadership/chazen-global-insights/symbolism-workplace-attire#:~:text=%E2%80%9CIt%20is%20the%20combination%20of,lens%20of%20power%20and%20status.

outside influences how you feel on the inside. Also, remember that looking good helps you develop money-making and socialising skills. When you look good, you feel good, and when you feel good, good things happen to you. As you look good, your confidence shines through in business meetings, negotiations, networking events and even in interviews. I have personally experienced this as most of my clients compliment me for my styling sense and fitness, asking me for shopping recommendations, too.

The key to building wealth is not only to think like the wealthy, but to act like one and eventually become one. The 'act as if' principle was popularised by Richard Wiseman and discovered by William James in 1880. It is based on the relationship between emotions and behaviour. Your emotions guide your behaviour. If you are feeling happy then you smile more, and if you feel sad then you frown more. In reverse, behaviour also can trigger emotions. For example, smiling can make you happy, and frowning can make you feel sad. The famous author Jack Canfield talked about this in his book *How To Get From Where You Are To Where You Want To Be: The 25 Principles Of Success*. His twelfth principle is on acting—thinking, talking, dressing, and feeling like a person who has already achieved his goals—and becoming a wealthy person. Acting, as if, sends powerful signals to your subconscious mind to find creative ways to achieve your goals.

So, in your journey to create wealth, remember to look and act wealthy so that you can become wealthy. Remember, be cautious and don't overdo it. Balance is important in all aspects of life.

Doctrine 19

Speculate To Accumulate

MANY A TIMES, we see successful people and think how lucky they are to have fame, money, and everything. But, we rarely see the hard work, struggle, dedication, discipline, and consistent efforts which they have put in to reach where they are today. Take the example of Sachin Tendulkar. He sacrificed his childhood and youth for cricket. He had played over 10,000 matches before playing for India which was not an easy task. You have to sacrifice many things to get what you want in life. You constantly and patiently keep doing your hard work and one day you will get what you want. But, you have to wait patiently for that one day before you reach your goal. You have to put in all your efforts, take all possible risks and bet everything for getting wealthy. Accept challenges and work around situations to reach your destination. You have to speculate so that one day you can accumulate. Here speculation does not refer to gambling or lottery, it means taking risks to reap real rewards. Speculative accumulation is also associated with investment as good returns only come from good investment.

The phrase 'speculate to accumulate' was first used by the English comic novelist P G Wodehouse when he said, 'If you don't speculate, you can't accumulate.' Wall Street also used this phrase occasionally pertaining to investment. For the accumulation of wealth, investment is necessary and for investment, one should understand the role of speculation. All investments are speculations but all speculations are not necessarily investments. Speculation is necessary and we all use it in investments. One can build wealth through investments, but the time involved depends on the goal of the investor. Since short-term trading cannot help in building huge wealth, long-term investments hold the key to building wealth and assets. You need to have a wealth mentality which can help in learning and improving your financial and investment skills. People with wealth mentality can take long-term speculative risks and are committed to achieving their financial goals, even if it means delayed gratifications.

Investments are simple yet boring and that's why it does not come easily. It requires a tremendous amount of patience. This doctrine—Speculate to Accumulate—can be considered saying that you have to accumulate to speculate to accumulate more. You need money in the first place to accumulate.

Doctrine 20

Risk Appetite

INVESTMENT PLANNING NEEDS calculated risk and for that one should ascertain their risk-taking capacity. Everyone has a different level of risk-taking capacity as it depends on age, goals, family environment, geographical location, religion, belief, and many other internal as well as external factors. It is important to know your risk appetite to plan your investment wisely. Risk appetite refers to the maximum amount of risk you are ready to take as an investor. For some investors, risk means excitement and opportunities, while for others it is discomfort and fear.

As an investor, you have to evaluate both risks and returns before investing. Shares and property are generally considered high-risk investments, though some bond and debt investments can also incur losses in the short-term. Hence, smart investors maintain a diverse investment portfolio for deciding the risk. To measure your risk appetite, you might need a good financial expert who can guide you as per your risk-taking capacity on your investments. If you have a high-risk appetite, you are willing to risk losing money now for the chance of making bigger gains later. If you have a low risk appetite you cannot take risks and lose money. A longer investment horizon lets you take more risk. Risk is inevitable in all types of investments, no matter whether you invest in stocks, crypto, bonds, or real estate. Risk means you lose money, break even, or earn money. Risk can be defined as an unfavourable or unexpected outcome. Since you are not 100 per cent sure about the outcome, some risk is involved. Not taking any risks means earning a steady but small profit; taking risks can either get you good returns or make you lose your money. So the solution is to maintain a balance. Keep a diverse portfolio that has a good mix of high, moderate, and no-risk investments. For designing a balanced portfolio, you need a financial expert. A financial expert will educate you on the various aspects of investments and guide you on risks based on your Return On Investment (ROI), financial goals, and risk appetite.

For understanding the significance of risk in investments, you should understand the three basic pillars of investment—Risk, Return, and Time. These three pillars lay the foundation of the investment strategy. The risk is dependent on the return you decide as per your goal and the period of the investment. You should consider the time period for your investment whether you want it short-term, mid-term, or long-term as per your goals, and based on that you can choose your investment options. Investing two things—your time and patience—are the most important. Remember, the time in the market is more important than timing the market, because the latter is not possible. Investment is not just about stocks; it consists of a variety of instruments that have varying degrees of risks and returns. You have to choose the right mix of investment tools as per your risk appetite, time duration, and goals. There is no magic formula for this. As per the research conducted by Brinson, Beebower, and Hood (1986), over 90 per cent of your portfolio's risk-adjusted returns is connected to your asset allocation.

As John Templeton famously said, 'The only investors who shouldn't diversify are those who are right one hundred per cent of the time.'

But the problem is that no one is right a hundred per cent of the time. To sum up, understand that it is up to you what level of risk you want to take. Risk has a lot to do with patience. It is a skill to be acquired, and not a talent. So, to cultivate patience one needs to work on financial literacy and learn the art of money management.

Doctrine 21

It's Never Late; Start Now

AT TIMES WE think that we started investing quite late in life. Had we started at a younger age, we would have earned a fortune by now. But believe me, it is never too late to start investing. Let's improvise one of our previous doctrines 'anybody can make money' to say—anybody can make money by investing at any age. It is never too late to start investing.

The only requirement is to focus on your goal and to invest following all the doctrines discussed in this book. If you need more money, focus on that alone because the more you focus on your goal, the easier your wealth-making journey becomes. You might have struggled a lot for earning money and creating wealth, but once you decide to earn more and get a clarity on your goals, then all the past struggle will cease to exist and you can then start afresh at any age, at any phase of your life. It is never ever late to start anything new in life, whether it is investment, acquiring new skills, starting new life all over again or any other thing.

We have a plenty of examples where people started off late and yet excelled in their pursuits. However, if you continue to think it is late, then it is. It is all in your belief. If you believe that you can achieve your goals at any age then, yes, you can. It is all about perception; all the hurdles for making money—age, sex, geography, skill level—can vanish if you start your investing journey with clear goals in mind.

'Wise spending is part of wise investing. And it's never too late to start.'—Rhonda Katz.

Investing now means taking advantage of the compounding returns as soon as possible. Compounding returns can be achieved with your ability to gain more over time by simply investing your profits into same/another investment instead of withdrawing it. This way your initial investment will grow faster than you can ever imagine. If you are starting to invest later in life then you have to ensure that you work strategically. While investing at an early age certainly gives an advantage of time, it is never too late to start. People nearing retirement are skeptical about investing as they find it scary and risky. The person who retires at the age of 60 has another 10 to 20 years of life during which they need to maintain their lifestyle, too, and that's why they need an investment strategy which suits their goals. Planning finances is a simple process, it needs discipline to fulfil goals, be it buying your dream home or enjoying early retirement life. Life is dynamic and financial goals keep changing. Financial planning will help you adopt these changes with requirements. Regular review of your financial planning with changing decision process will help you make a priority change that will align your financial goals with the current life situation. You are never too young or old to start investing.

Remember that even if you invest a small amount, it can eventually make a huge difference when compounding over years. Cash cannot keep up with inflation. Today life expectancy is increasing, and people are living longer so investment is also becoming more important.

Doctrine 22

Financial Needs Are Dynamic

HUMAN LIFE IS always undergoing change. As a teenager, we have a different mindset and need, which, later, from adulthood to old age, again keeps shifting. When we are young, we are carefree, but once we get married we start taking responsibility and after becoming parents we get more serious in fulfilling our duties. Around the age of 55, we tend to get more spiritual as we detach from our responsibilities. As per our age, our focus, strategy, needs, and responsibilities keep changing. Our financial needs also change over time based on the age and stage of our life. What choices we make and what kind of lifestyle we have also make a difference to our financial needs. So it is clear that with age, our financial planning needs to change.

'Financial planning is like navigation. If you know where you are and where you want to go, navigation isn't such a great problem. It's when you don't know the two points that it's difficult.'—Venita VanCaspel.

With proper financial planning, you can optimally use your income. Contrary to the dynamic financial needs, there are two things that remain constant across all age groups—taxation and contingencies. That's why it is advisable to opt for some tax-efficient strategies. You have to keep some reserves for contingency and emergency. Planning with these things in mind is indispensable. Make provision for emergency funds and secure enough insurance coverage for yourself and those dependent on you. You have to keep checking where you are, where you would like to reach and what will be your need in the future. A financial planner needs to answer three basic questions:
- What is your current financial standing?
- Where do you want to be tomorrow?
- What do you need to do to reach your destination?

There is a 4-points checklist that you should follow before planning your finance:
- Keep track of your income and expenses.
- Identify and prioritise your goals.
- Design your investment plan.
- Check the different investment avenues.

A careful financial planning will help you deal with inflation, retirement fund, and upgrading and maintaining your lifestyle. With a thoroughly chalked out financial plan you can know where you stand and where you want to go.

Doctrine 23

Art Of Negotiation And Deal-Making

GOOD DEALS CAN make you rich, and to bag such deals, you need to learn the art of negotiation. What attributes or skills you have that others might want? Analyse your skills, virtues, possessions, and knowledge that can be traded and swapped. Many rich people have accumulated wealth by trading their skills and knowledge. And when you strike a good deal, everybody feels happy with the outcome. You can study the story of Straw Millionaire, a Japanese Buddhist folk, who became wealthy with a series of successful trades, starting with a single price of straw. You can also refer to a website created by a Canadian blogger, Kyle MacDonald, who traded a single red paper clip[5]. with a house in a series of 14 online

---

5   YouTube *What if you could trade a paperclip for a house?* [Online] Retrieved from: https://www.youtube.com/watch?app=desktop&si=_uet_KNnOdv-GAytq&v=8s3bdVxuFBs&feature=youtu.be

trades over a year. Kyle MacDonald was inspired by the game Bigger, Better.

All these stories are nothing but the best examples of the art of negotiation and deal-making. Developing your negotiation skills can be a big step ahead in your financial journey. Not negotiating means leaving the money on the table.

Negotiation helps you earn more money and get great deals when making purchases, thereby helping you tackle financial challenges. To acquire these skills, you can refer to books and blogs and practice those skills. Some of these skills are basic and are based on human psychology. These are:

- Be a good listener.
- Always know your bottom line.
- Be clear about what you want.
- Have a flexible mindset.
- Ask more questions.
- Master the timing and be clear about when to strike deal.
- Be confident at all level of negotiations.
- Practice win-win theory.
- Be emphatic always.
- Master your communication skills.
- Be ready to walk away.
- Offer options.
- Be clear on what matters the most.
- Do your research and homework.
- Don't make concessions.
- Create more values for your offers.
- Know in details what they want.
- Avoid anxiety.
- Be considerate.

So master your skills in deal-making and negotiations as these will help you in all spheres of life, like relationship, business and in creating wealth. To conclude, let's go back to the basic rules—

- Know what you are getting.
- Why is it important to you.
- What is expected from you.
- What are you expecting.
- What are they getting.
- Where do you want to end up.
- Where they want to end up.

Be clear on the above points and see, you will love all aspects of deal-making and negotiations. Cracking deals and coming up with negotiations can get easier if you keep this checklist handy.

Doctrine 24

Spend Less Than What You Earn

LET'S TALK ABOUT the one golden rule that everyone should follow. You must have some savings with which you can generate more income. We must learn to live within our means, but live well enough to be happy. If you cannot afford a five-star dinner daily, then have it at least a month if that's what makes you happy. But, remember to save by all means. The biggest bottleneck in creating wealth is not knowing what you are doing, where you are standing financially and where are you heading. You have to be in control of your financial situation if you want to create wealth. You should know your income and spending so that you can boost the former and curb the latter. You should be well aware of your future expenses and emergency requirements so that you can plan the contingency fund. You should also be well aware of any future income that you might be getting. People often go wrong in not knowing themselves financially well. Go into the micro-details to understand your finances—your earning per month, per week, per day, per hour. You should be aware of your spending habits; know your cost of living. Do you buy unnecessary things, or do you spend on impulse? Do you tend to waste your money? Do you spend wisely? Do you negotiate before buying? Do you respect money? All these points are pertinent when it comes to financial planning.

There is a saying that cutting out your daily cappuccino isn't going to make you rich, which is correct, but partly. We also have a saying, penny-wise, but pound-foolish. Cutting down too much on the necessities will make you miserable and not rich.

You need the necessities of life that empower you to earn more. Save money, plan your finances, but don't deprive yourself of the little pleasures of life that enrich your life, making it more meaningful. Don't waste money, but don't hesitate before spending it on yourself. If you can't afford what you want, buy less, but, buy quality. Giving up little luxuries of life will not help you create wealth. It will trap you in the poverty cycle.

To conclude, let's turn to the famous interview of the legendary Warren Buffett with CNBC, where he said, 'Success is doing what you love and doing it well. It is as simple as that. Getting to do what you love to do every day, that's the ultimate luxury. Your standard of living is not equal to your cost of living.'

Remember, your destiny, like your money, is in your hands. Maintain a balance between your earning and spending. Spend less than what you earn, and strive to earn more to keep your spending within a check.

Doctrine 25

Don't Borrow Or Consolidate Debts

WHOEVER LENDS MONEY, they want it back with interest and more. If not urgent, don't ever borrow. If you have to borrow at all, then chalk out a plan to pay it off as soon as possible. Remember, when you borrow, you not only have to pay interest but compromise on your respect, and, sometimes, your relationships, too.

There is no such thing as free money. Borrowing makes you weak; it may trap you into a habit of continuous borrowing. You cannot create wealth with borrowed money. You have to understand that if you borrow money, you have to pay interest, emotions, happiness, and goodwill. Pay off all your loans and debts before you do anything else.

However, it is undeniable that to start a business, you have to borrow. But, you need to calculate the cost and create a plan to pay it off. Do not ever borrow if you do not have a well-thought-out plan. Also, be cautious against converting your short-term debt into a long-term one. By all means, consolidate all your debts.

Before you make your mind to borrow, please consider some of the basic points:
- If you have a chance to consolidate all your debts, negotiate and seize the opportunity.
- Don't mortgage your home ever.
- Check for an early settlement clause.
- Pay off as early as possible.
- Always borrow against an asset that you can resell and never borrow more than the resale value.

However, not all debts are bad. Good debt, like home loans, helps you get assets that gain in value and add to your wealth.

Keep credit cards only if you can pay within the stipulated time period. Don't waste money paying interest. Your first step towards your wealth quest should be to get loans/debts paid off as soon as possible. There is no point in depositing money in a savings bank account for 7-8 per cent interest while paying for a loan at 10-12 per cent interest rate.

Although it is difficult to be debt-free, you must prioritise it. Make a plan for consolidating debts/paying off loans and stick to it. If you have more than one loan, start by paying off the one with the highest interest. It is a short-term pain for long-term gain, so keep yourself motivated to pay off loans.

Once you're debt-free, make a resolution to never go back.

The proverb 'quick to borrow is always slow to pay' stands true in this context. Make sure you are not accumulating debt as you march towards your goal of creating wealth. In case, you really need to borrow ever, be quick to pay it off.

Doctrine 26

Understand What Is Investment

MOST INVESTMENTS HAVE a dual nature—they generate income while appreciating in value. When you invest, you receive a regular interest along with the increase in the actual value of your investment.

In real estate sector, if you've invested in a property and rented it out, you can earn regular rent while the property's value continues to appreciate. Likewise, an investment in shares can yield dividends and also lead to the appreciation of your shares' value.

> 'Successful investing is about managing risk, not avoiding it.'—Benjamin Graham

Investing does involve an element of risk as you can incur losses as well. A well-diversified portfolio of low-risk investments can offer decent returns, too.

Investment is an asset created with the intention of

growing money. The wealth generated through investment can be used for various purposes such as retirement, meeting financial shortages, loan repayments, asset purchases, or paying for education or health requirements etc. Depending on your needs, you can set long-term goals and plan investments accordingly.

Understanding investments thoroughly is crucial. Choosing the right investment depends on your goals, current financial situation, and risk tolerance. Successful investment requires a long-term vision, discipline, patience, consistency, planning, and determination. It involves winning small battles on the journey to achieve success in the end.

There are numerous options to invest into:
- Equity
- Antiques
- Arts
- Bonds
- Mutual Funds
- Gold
- PPF (Public Provident Fund)
- Intellectual Property (IP)
- Films/Serials/Theatre Shows
- Angel Capital
- Sponsorships
- Sports
- Talents
- Cryptocurrency

Before investing, it is essential to consider several key factors. These can include your financial needs and goals, the importance of diversifying your investments, and the time period you plan to invest for. Equally crucial is understanding the purpose of investment. The purpose will vary and might include ensuring safety, leveraging the compounding effect for money growth, creating steady and multiple income streams, minimising tax liabilities, and planning for retirement. By keeping these considerations in mind, you can make informed investment decisions that align with your financial objectives.

> 'The most important quality for an investor is temperament, not intellect. You need a temperament that neither derives great pleasure from being with the crowd, nor from going against it.'—Warren Buffet.

Understand investments clearly to maximise your gains.
- Investment involves using capital today to increase its value over time.
- Investment requires putting capital to work, in the form of time, money, efforts etc., to generate a future pay off which is greater than the initial investment.
- Investments usually do not come with guarantees of appreciation; they may yield low returns.
- Investment needs diversification to reduce risk.

Though individual talent can contribute to investment success, a collective effort gives better results. A financial advisor can help with long-term investing, diversifying your holdings across different asset classes. Diversification provides portfolio stability, balancing risk and rewards and can avoid impulsive decisions. Investors must address the fear and greed syndrome to steer clear of this.

While savings are for accumulating money, investing is for growing money. Investing is all about generating real return and never about chasing the highest return. Post-tax rate of return which is greater than the rate of inflation is termed as Real Return.

To conclude, know your investment options and consider their return value. Weigh your options and make an informed decision that can help you grow your money and achieve your money-goals.

Doctrine 27

Build Capital And Invest Wisely

MOST OF US get confused with our money when our earnings improve. Once you start earning well, you might want to spend it on yourself and your family, as that's indeed one of the intended purposes. However, be cautious and don't overspend! No matter how badly you wish to buy your dream house, car, or other luxuries, exercise self-control. I know many people who, after suddenly receiving a substantial amount from selling their land at an attractive price, failed to manage that sum. They began buying unnecessary luxuries without any investments and ended up squandering it all.

We must understand the role of delayed gratification and the importance of building wealth. Starting your journey toward wealth creation requires some initial capital. Just as street performers put some money in their hat to encourage others to contribute, you also need to set aside a lump sum whenever you can. Once you've accumulated enough capital, you can invest it in promising investment opportunities.

The goal is to transform your funds into assets that generate additional revenue, whether through property, shares, or other avenues. Wealth accrues gradually as you channel your surplus amount into investments that work in your favour.

For investing, the first step is to determine your surplus income. This could be the money saved regularly or the funds previously allocated to housing loan but now redirected towards SIPs (Systematic Investment Plans). Surplus income refers to any money left over after covering your monthly expenses. It could stem from a bonus, dividend, or inheritance. Such surplus funds are ideal for investment, as saving alone might not provide a retirement corpus capable of combating inflation.

These surplus funds can be invested across a range of options in accordance with your goals and risk tolerance. To grow your accessible funds and achieve prosperity, it's essential to steer away from conventional investment avenues like traditional savings. Instead, channel your surplus money into mutual funds, portfolio management services, and alternate investment funds among others.

The act of saving and investing money regularly will significantly change the way you live your life in the future. So, cultivate the habit of generating surplus funds to enable investment and wealth creation. With investments that work in your favour, you will soon reach your goal and amass wealth.

Doctrine 28

Equity Versus Property

CREATING WEALTH NEEDS various strategies and investment options where both equity and property play a vital role. Equity investments in stocks or businesses offer the potential for higher returns but it has higher volatility in price. Property investments, such as real estate, can provide a steady income through rental earnings and property value appreciation. Limited investment in property is low liquidity and requires large amount to invest. It is easy to buy property but difficult to sell. The choice between property and equity depends on factors like your risk-appetite, investment goals, market conditions, and personal preferences.

Diversification across different asset classes is a perfect approach to managing risk for creating wealth. Consulting a financial expert can help design a customised strategy as per your goal with the preference of property versus equity.

In my opinion, in the longer run, equity tends to outperform property. Nonetheless, your portfolio should have property investment too. One big advantage of investing in property is that it gives you a sense of ownership because it is a tangible asset. With property, you can plan a good rental income that can keep coming. I know one client who has planned and bought some multi-storied buildings in metro cities, leasing them out to reputed corporate companies, thereby generating a good amount of passive income. But for that, you need a well-planned strategy as real estate is a risky proposition. You need to do your homework in depth before buying. Check the details like ownership proof, compliance and other legal formalities. Don't forget that majority of disputes in courts are civil litigations. It is not a one-time work; maintenance, compliance, transfer are recurring work even after acquiring ownership.

With shares, you keep getting dividends at regular intervals, and in the long run, your share value can appreciate considerably. You can get the benefit of bonus shares and preference shares, too. Indian equity market is highly regulated and customer safety is a prime concern for the regulator. Though it is easier to manage, one needs to be updated on regular basis with regard to review, research, and nominations among other things. Property has a geographical limitation; it is not easy to buy, own and maintain a property far away from your local area since physical visits are needed from time to time. Both property and shares values can go down too, but if invested wisely in equity, the chances of value appreciation are higher. Moreover, in shares you can deviate your risk by having multiple categories of companies' shares. The more variety you have, the less risky it gets. While equity investment can give immediate liquidity, selling real estate properties at

good rates need time and patience. You can sell a fraction of your equity but selling a fraction of a single property is not feasible. Equity investment can create wealth as several key factors contribute to its potential for significant returns:
- Long Term Growth Potential
- Compound Interest
- Ownership in Profitable Companies
- Diversification
- Liquidity
- Inflation Hedge

It is noteworthy that while equity investments offer potential for wealth creation, they also come with risks, including market volatility and ending up owning poor or bad companies. You need a good financial expert who can guide you and design your portfolio for mutual funds or offer Portfolio Management Services (PMS) to create wealth.

We can conclude by saying that investment in the equity market requires a lot of research and regular market update which is not possible for people who are not from the finance field. One needs to commit time as mastering the art of equity investment requires years of practice and dedication. A good financial expert can keep you updated with market trends and help you to make well-informed decisions that maximise your potential for wealth creation.

Doctrine 29

Master The Technique Of Selling

BEHIND EVERY WEALTHY person is his unique art of selling. In every aspect of life, you have to exhibit this skill, either in selling yourself or in selling your skills, products or services. The more you sell, the more you earn. A good idea is useless if not sold well. You cannot make money without selling. Every rich person knows this well and every poor person is poor because of failing in this.

So, it is imperative that you master the art of selling. Sell even when you are sleeping; sell into the places where you have never been. Use your contacts and sell on the foreign shores.

Some of the things you can try selling are:
- Yourself
- Your skills
- Unique products/services
- Products/services offered by others
- Products/services that are in high demand

You can brainstorm and find out which product or services you should sell to create wealth.

People failed in selling because they tried selling the products which nobody wanted. Don't be shy of selling yourself because you are also a brand. Observe how Richard Branson is selling himself. You need one idea or one unique product to change your fortune.

Mastering the art of selling involves understanding the customer's needs, good communication skills, networking abilities, passion for marketing and the ability to convey the benefits of your product/service while addressing the objections too. Continuous practice and learning from experiences can make you a good salesperson. Remember, for selling you don't need to be a salesperson. You should be able to offer genuine value to customers, identify their pain points and provide solution to their problems. For a good sale, you have to be consistent, understand market trends, and refine your selling strategies. You also have to be ethical and careful about environmental issues pertaining to your products and services because ethical and customer-centric approach can give you the best results in long run.

Selling is fundamental to earning money in many business endeavours. There are many examples of famous salespersons who made billions. One example is Mary Kay Ash. She founded Mary Kay Cosmetics in 1963 and employed her sales skills to build a successful direct sales business. Her company's innovative sales model empowered women to become independent beauty consultants and motivated them to make millions. Another individual who made millions through sales is Shiv Nadar. He is the founder of HCL Technologies, a multinational IT services and consulting company. His ability to sell IT services to global clients played a pivotal role in building HCL Technologies into a multi-billion dollar business and establishing him as one of India's wealthiest individuals.

You can refer to the success stories of brands like Pan Parag, Parle, Infosys, Reliance, and Tata among others, where an individual has created wealth using impeccable selling techniques.

So, get back to the basics; follow ethical selling practices. Brush up on your selling skills to stride ahead in your wealth-creating journey. Tell your customers how your product/service can benefit them. Remember, with a good sale comes good money.

Doctrine 30

Learn To Lose So You Can Win

NOT ONLY IN wealth creation but in life too you should learn to lose in order to win. Many of us overlook the crucial aspects of the journey—the ability to embrace losses as valuable learning opportunities. It is the failures and losses which give us valuable insights and instil resilience necessary to achieve prosperity. Learning to lose in order to win is a fundamental principle that can lead to creation of wealth.

Failures and set backs are inevitable in all phases of journey. All the great entrepreneurs and winners have learnt how to face losses and overcome failures to achieve the desired results. The key here is the shift in the mindset—from viewing losses as defeats to seeing them as stepping stones, and finally to victory.

We have to consider following points for understanding this doctrine:
- **Consider all Failures as Feedback Streams:**
  Losing in business of investments gives valuable feedback as it provides an opportunity to analyse what went wrong.

It follows the trial–and-error approach whereby the investor can refine the investment strategy, mitigate risks and increase the probability of success.

- **Cultivate Resilience, Adaptability and Flexibility:**
Experiencing losses cultivates resilience and adaptability which are the most desirable traits in investment. Learning to bounce back from failure with a positive mindset helps to cultivate resilience. Resilience plays an important role in attaining investment success. Persistence will prove to be another indispensable quality in this journey.

- **Calculated Risk-Taking:**
Calculated risk-taking plays an important role in creating wealth. Embracing the possibility of loss while striving for the gains allows for more informed decision-making. Risk management is an art which helps in minimising potential losses and maximising gains over time.

- **Gain Knowledge and Expertise:**
Losing comes with many incentives and one of these is gaining a depth of insight and knowledge which subsequently increases the expertise. You can learn from your mistakes and work on yourself to get rid of them. Seek advice from your mentors, financial advisors or by referring to books. Attend webinars, meetings and seminars on the subject as learning is a continuous process. Learn how to make informed decisions and control your fear and greed.

- **Long-term Vision and Patience:**
The journey towards wealth is not a sprint but a marathon. Learning to lose and patiently working upon your goals reinforces the importance of a long-term vision. You

should not be discouraged by the immediate setbacks. Stay focused on your goals and keep working to achieve them.

- **Fear of Failure:**
  The fear of failures always dissuades one from attempting new things and taking calculated risk. Once you are comfortable with the idea of losing, you can take calculated risks and opt for more challenging investment options. Once the fear of losing is out of the door, you can seize newer opportunities which you might have missed otherwise.

- **Persistence is the Key:**
  Persistent efforts even in the face of adversity hold the key to success. Those who learn to lose graciously can refine their strategies and emerge as a winner at the end.

'You can't let your failures define you. You have to let your failures teach you.' –Barack Obama.

Learning to lose in order to win is nothing but transforming your mindset and knowing that if you want to win you need to learn to face losses. Most of the great investors learn from their mistakes and move on, while the retail investors cling to bad investments and keep losing their money. As per Warren Buffet, the essence of selling loss-making investments is a part of wealth management. He advises investors to be flexible and to reassess their strategies when faced with a loss-making investment. He famously stated, 'You don't have to make it back the way you lost it,' emphasising the importance of moving funds to more promising opportunities rather than holding onto the failing ones. Similarly, Buffett's advice to 'stop digging' when in a hole highlights the wisdom of cutting losses and avoiding further financial damage. These principles underscore the necessity of adaptability and prudent decision-making in investment management.

Remember, if you want to win in life, learn to lose. With every loss and failure you gain better knowledge and insight. With perseverance and consistency, you learn to take calculated risks and master the art of investing.

Doctrine 31

Understand The Stock Market Before Buying

STOCK BUYING GIVES ownership equity in the firm and allows the shareholders voting rights as well as a residual claim on corporate earnings in the form of capital gains and dividends.

Individual and institutional investors come together on stock exchanges to buy and sell shares. Share prices are set by supply and demand as buyers and sellers place orders, and by the underlying business fundamentals like profit growth, governance, etc.

Now, the most pertinent question that arises is how to master this trade? The simple answer is, buy low, sell high. However, there is more to stock investing. What to buy, how much to buy, when to buy, when to sell—there are innumerable books and literature available on this subject. Though complex, you need to understand the basics, like value and speculations.

John Maynard Keynes famously quoted, 'Stock market is just like a beauty contest.'

This refers to the opinion poll and voting patterns. Whoever is voted by the opinion poll can win. Similarly, the stock preferred by the most will rise and that leaves everything to speculation. Investors try to make money by buying stocks they think other investors want to buy in the future, and the price depends less on fundamentals of the company than the future anticipation and that's where the speculations come into play.

If you want to make money from the stock market then go slowly, but surely. Ignore the noise, speculation, and grapevine. Think long-term. Resist the urge to make quick money from stock market. Resist all technical analysis and tools. Look for the companies that make or do something that people will find more valuable in the future. Go for the companies whose value might be appreciated by the institutional investors. Find good stocks and buy them for long-term, unless the fundamentals get changed. Equally important is to keep adding to the position over time as the underlying business grows and becomes more valuable. Rakesh Jhunjhunwala, often referred to as Indian's Warren Buffett, is best known for his conviction and the size of position in an individual stock. He made fortune not just by identifying Titan Company well ahead of others, but his conviction to build large size in the said stock over time. So, wait for the appreciation and see your wealth increasing.

Buy the right stocks at the right prices. Don't follow the crowd, rather follow the value. All these needs a lot of research. Cut the odds down as low as possible and invest in things you understand. It's better to buy mutual funds or seek advice from a financial expert. If you don't have the time to research, you should have an investment advisor. There are many investment options related to stock market which they can suggest. However, know some basics before investing in stock market:

- Buy the right stocks.
- Create a diversified portfolio.
- Have Patience, think long-term and be ready for the downturn.
- Practice. One needs to have lifetime commitment towards learning.
- Build long-term portfolio, and avoid short-term impulses.
- Stay invested; it is the time in market and not timing the market that will build wealth.

> 'The stock market is a device for transferring money from the impatient to the patient.' –Warren Buffett

Remember that investing in stock market involves risk and there is no guarantee of profit. You must make a well-informed decision before buying in stock market. Never make active equity trading the source of your primary income (earnings). One of the most important skills is cultivating the right temperament and intention to build wealth from equity and not take an easy shortcut to make quick money.

Doctrine 32

Create Multiple Streams Of Income

ALL THE RICH people in the world have more than one income source. Observe the wealthy around you; you will notice that they have diversified their investments and income sources to create prosperity. If one income source slows down or closes, other sources can compensate for their income stream. Similarly, you have to keep looking for multiple income sources to create wealth.

Having multiple sources of income is important for several reasons, such as:

- **Risk Diversification:** Depending only on one source of income is risky. If you lose your job or your primary income source stops due to some reasons, then you have to face financial hardship. Multiple sources of income can help you face such situations.
- **Building Savings and Investments:** Extra income allows you to save more and invest more. This helps you build up your investment portfolio so that you can generate more compounding returns.

- **Financial Stability:** Multiple income streams provide a safety net during emergencies, economic downturns, medical emergencies, or unexpected fund requirements.
- **Wealth Acceleration:** Money begets money. When you have more money to invest, your wealth grows at a faster rate. You can take more risks when you have multiple sources of income.
- **Entrepreneurship Opportunities:** Multiple sources of income can give you a chance to invest in promising projects and business opportunities, leading to more wealth creation.
- **Lifestyle Options:** Multiple sources of income enable you to live a Financial Freedom Lifestyle, giving you a flexibility and allowing you to make choices aligned with your lifestyle goals, such as early retirement or pursuing your passion.
- **Wealth Preservation:** Multiple sources of income help you create and even protect your wealth. If one source of income is affected, the other sources keep you moving toward wealth creation and protection.

In short, multiple streams of income provide financial security, growth opportunities, and the ability to create wealth more rapidly, which are essential aspects of wealth creation.

There are many examples of rich people who have created multiple sources of income and, by doing so, have amassed wealth. Creating passive income can diversify the risk and create wealth. All this showcases how creating wealth through multiple sources of income streams, including investments, entrepreneurship, and diversified business interests, can lead to financial success. These people have unique abilities to adapt, innovate, and leverage their resources across various sectors, and that's the secret behind their wealth.

You should know how to turn cash into assets that work for you and bring passive income. I know a businessman who has invested part of his income from one source into another source—real estate—and created a portfolio of offices in all metro cities of India. He then rents out these offices to corporations, creating a huge passive income. Rent from property is one example, and annual dividends from shares are another. Another person I know, has built an equity portfolio over time to generate dividend and gain income equivalent to his company's fixed costs, such as salaries, wages and utilities. This helped in building a strong distribution-network pan India giving a significant entry barrier to his competitors.

You have to create new income streams by finding ways to use your skills and expertise in more than one setting. However, what your primary income source is and how you can maintain it are also crucial. Your income is what makes you rich and it will never be enough no matter how much your income increases. The more you earn, the higher the work insecurities and stress. To attain financial freedom one needs to build multiple sources of income, the majority being passive.

Your key takeaway from this doctrine would be to maximise all your skills to bring in income and then actively invest in assets that will get you money. You need not do everything yourself; focus on your core expertise and outsource the other skills. Money flowing in from multiple directions will strengthen the foundation of your finances.

Doctrine 33

Play 'What If' To Create Wealth

'WHAT IF' IS A thinking in psychology often used in scenario planning or strategic foresight and plays a significant role in the creation of wealth. This style of thinking can be helpful in many ways, such as:

- Risk Mitigation: 'What If' scenarios help identify potential risks and challenges that could impact your wealth creation strategies. By considering various situations and options, you can develop contingency plans to mitigate various risks involved, which helps create and protect your wealth.
- Exploration of Various Opportunities: 'What If' thinking can also help identify untapped opportunities through situational analysis and decision-making regarding investment options. You may discover different avenues for income generation or investments that you may not have considered previously.
- Innovation and Adaptation: Wealth creation involves adapting to changing circumstances and markets. 'What If' thinking encourages innovation and flexibility by

helping you think and explore how various wealth-building options can help create wealth in different situations.
- **Long-Term Thinking and Planning:** Wealth creation is a journey with many steps; it is a long-term process and cannot be completed overnight. 'What If' thinking helps you plan for the future, anticipate trends, and develop adaptability and flexibility as per the situation.
- **Asset Allocation:** It helps you decide which assets can withstand the 'What If' situations. It helps you assess the economic situation, political stability, and market dynamics affecting your portfolio, allowing you to fine-tune your investment portfolio accordingly.
- **Crucial Decisions:** 'What If' thinking can help you make informed decisions in almost all situations in life.

'What If' thinking is a valuable investment tool as it encourages wealth creation and protection by considering various situations. With this thinking tool, you can analyse all scenarios and make informed and resilient decisions, ensuring wealth creation.

When deciding how to earn money and where to invest your money, you have to ask many questions starting with 'What If', like:
- What if the market crashes?
- What if the returns do not meet expectations?
- What if the gold price goes down?
- What if the sector in which I have invested does not perform well?
- What if the real estate market experiences a recession? What if...

Diversification is the name of the game, and 'What If' is the tool with which you can play this game successfully. Remember, wealth creation is as much about smart investing and earning as it is about calculating the risk factors and tackling them efficiently. With the right approach, that is the 'what if' perspective, one can foresee the potential threats and be better prepared to battle them.

Doctrine 34

Money Making Is Not A Secret, Learn The Art

MONEY MAKING IS not a secret. It is an art that you need to learn and implement. Wealth creation typically involves doctrines such as saving, investing, and making informed financial decisions repeatedly. It's not a secret, but requires discipline, knowledge, and a long-term perspective.

It's all about understanding how money works and how you can adapt to the changing circumstances. Continuous learning and practice can help you become adept in this art.

The doctrine of wealth creation involves various principles and strategies aimed at building and managing wealth. Though there is no single universal doctrine; some common rules include:

- **Financial Education:** Developing a strong understanding of personal finances, including budgeting, saving, investing, and debt management, is crucial. We all should learn these basic financial rules and teach them to our children, as no school or university covers this.

- **Goal Setting:** I can't emphasise this enough. The first step in wealth creation is clearly defining financial goals, both short-term and long-term, and creating a plan to achieve them.
- **Income Generation:** Focusing on increasing your income through various sources and means, such as employment, entrepreneurship, and investment, is essential.
- **Savings and Investment:** Consistently saving a portion of your income and investing it wisely in assets that have the potential to grow over time is the key to achieving financial freedom.
- **Diversification:** Spreading your investments across different asset classes to reduce risk and enhance returns is important.
- **Risk Management:** Understanding and managing the risks associated with investments and financial decisions can keep you on track during your wealth creation journey.
- **Long-Term Perspective:** Wealth creation takes time and requires patience and discipline.
- **Continuous Learning:** Since economic conditions are always dynamic, constant learning is necessary.
- **Giving Back:** You should give it back to get it back. Philanthropy and contribution to causes you care about will give you inner peace and a feeling of accomplishment.

Wealth creation is an individual journey that differs from person to person based on various circumstances. It's essential to tailor your approach as per your unique situation and continue to adapt as required.

No one other than you can help you get wealthy. There

are no shortcuts, and you should stay away from get-rich-quick schemes. Lazy people do not get rich, rather they end up poor because they look for shortcuts.

So, let's gear up to walk on the challenging path of wealth creation with dedication, perseverance, and discipline.

Doctrine 35

Become Wealthy By Implementing

YES, THIS IS true. *Money Management Doctrine* is the result of three generations of wisdom accumulated from observing and learning from many wealthy people, including my wealthy clients, and the crux of the principles followed by many great achievers.

If you have observed, I have tried to reiterate and emphasise many basic traits of money-making so that these get engraved onto your mind. Though you might find them quite basic, these simple rules can make a world of difference. You may also say that you know them already, but have you implemented them? That's the catch—knowing and executing are different. You cannot achieve anything merely by knowing the secrets to money-making.

Knowing and implementing are two distinct but interconnecting concepts. Knowing is a prerequisite for effective implementation. You need to know how to do something and understand the concept before implementing it. However, knowledge alone does not guarantee successful implementation. The ability to implement effectively often depends on factors such as skills, resources, motivation, and discipline.

Implementing everything learnt here requires mental shifts as most of the concepts are psychological and belief-oriented. You have to start implementing these doctrines gradually but consistently. You might have to change yourself and your beliefs. Developing new character traits is always difficult, but you have to face it with determination.

You have to change your mindset. You have to change the way you behave and talk about money. Do you consider money as good or evil? The way you change your behaviour regarding money will start showing results rapidly. Begin by changing your awareness of what money is and what it can do for you. Money myths influence everything in wealth creation. Your confidence and determination also play a great role. You have to uplift your image and behave and think like a wealthy person. Act as if you are rich. When you start behaving like a rich person, your perception changes and you start attracting wealthy thoughts.

Effective implementation is an interactive process and requires ongoing consistent efforts and refinement. The key is to bridge the gap between knowing and doing by taking purposeful and strategic actions based on your acquired knowledge. Knowledge acquired but never implemented is an absolute waste of resources. Make sure you do not waste yours!

Doctrine 36

Listen To Your Intuition

DEVELOP THE SKILLS to listen to your inner voice. Intuitive skills are useful in making decisions.

You might have experienced that right before finalising a deal your intuition starts warning you against it. Listen to that intuition and don't proceed with that deal.

If you don't trust someone, don't do business with them. Trust is the most fundamental part for cultivating business ties.

If you don't trust your financial advisor and your intuition asks you to change him, do it immediately. If you don't trust your boss, don't work for him. If you don't have trust in relationships, leave them.

Similarly, listen to your intuition when it comes to wealth. Intuition often draws on your sub conciliatory knowledge and experiences. Let's see how:

- **Self-awareness:** Understand your financial goals, values and risk tolerance. Intuition is most reliable when aligned with your personal aspirations.

- **Financial Education:** The more you know about investments, savings, and financial strategies, the better your intuition can guide you.
- **Past Experience:** Your intuition is influenced by your past experiences.
- **Catch The Signals:** Pay attention to the subtle signals your intuition sends, catch them and trust them to take actions.
- **Risk Analysis:** Intuition will help you to analyse the risk involved in any situation, whether financial or personal.
- **Patience:** Intuition will guide you when to wait or act. Patience and right timing is important for wealth building and intuition will help with that.
- **Balance Reasoning with Intuition:** You have to learn the art of combining your intuition with the reasoning and balance them based on your financial knowledge and experiences. You can use facts and data to complement your intuition and make the right financial decision. Be wary of pre-determined outcomes. The whole exercise needs to be open ended without bias or defined conclusion.
- **Constant Learning:** Keeping yourself abreast with the latest trends and continuous learning and adapting is necessary to make the most effective use of your intuition. Your intuition evolves as you gain more experiences and knowledge, so always be receptive to new information.

Intuition is a powerful tool; it is vital to strike a balance with informed decision-making to navigate the complexities of wealth building effectively.

Intuition is the compass guiding wealth building; it whispers insights beyond numbers, steering decisions with a wisdom that transcends the ledger. Make a note of what your gut feeling says. Give your intuition a free wheel.

Doctrine 37

Start The Investments Early

I HAVE MISSED the bus! Yes, I did not invest when I was young, so I have made it a point to teach my children to start investing at an early age.

I have designed an innovative piggy bank named after my investment company Jumbo and gifted it to many as it is the best way to educate children on saving and how the saved amounts can be invested smartly. It is the duty of every parent to teach their children about investment.

Saving is a golden habit and we all must cultivate it. Many a times I think had I started investing early, my portfolio might have been more than doubled by now.

Nonetheless, I am happy as both of my children are saving since their young age and they understand the value of money.

But why is it beneficial to start investing from an early age?

- **Compounding Growth:** The early you start investing, the more your money grows through compounding. You will earn returns not only on your initial investment but also on returns generated on previous periods.

- **Risk Tolerance:** Starting early will give you a longer period of investment which means you can take more risk. Riskier investments often give higher potential returns, and with time on your side, you can withstand market fluctuations.
- **Learning Curve:** Starting early allows you to learn more, gain experience, learn from mistakes and refine your investment strategy over time.
- **Financial Discipline:** Investing from an early age and doing it consistently will help you form a habit that can encourage financial discipline. Ultimately, a financial discipline will help you create wealth.
- **Diversification:** Early investment will give you a chance to diversify your portfolio, spreading risk across different asset classes. This will help you protect your investments during the market downturns.
- **Long-term Goals:** An early investment gives you an opportunity to fulfil your long-term financial goals.

Early investment habits will give you many advantages. Start early and teach your children to start an early investment. Plant the seeds of your financial future early, and watch your investments grow into the mighty oaks of prosperity.

Doctrine 38

Work Hard To Get Rich

THE JOURNEY TOWARDS getting rich involves a lot of hard work and sacrifice. You cannot live like an average person does. You have to work longer hours, skip the normal routine and work passionately towards fulfilling your long-term goals.

You might have to work on Sundays, letting go of weekend movies or your favourite show on television. You might have to skip a friends' get together or a marriage function of your near and dear one. Long lunch breaks, short weekend tours, hanging out with friends, and all other leisurely activities have to be sacrificed if you want to be rich. We know that money doesn't grow on trees; one needs to work hard to earn it enough. Once you are rich, the money works for you.

See all the rich and successful people who have created good wealth. What do they do? They are always busy with their schedule so that they can achieve their self-determined financial goals.

Dedication, discipline and consistency, together with the

conviction for your financial goals, will help you to achieve financial independence. If you are not serious towards your financial goals, then this journey is not for you. If you are not ready to work hard then this destination can never be reached. If you are not disciplined then no money doctrine can help you to get rich.

You have to undertake this journey with a passion. With a burning passion to get rich, all the hard work and sacrifice would seem easy. Blend your hard work with smart work. Only doing hard work cannot make you rich.

You have to work like you have never worked before; you have to work like your life depends on it. You have to decide why you need money, what are your short, medium and long-term goals and how are you going to achieve them. Hard work with smart planning is the key to get results.

You have to work upon your strategies, ideas and goals for getting rich. You might have a good business idea and some money to start it, but you still need to put in hard and smart work to make it happen.

For getting rich, you are required to put in significant effort and dedication. Working hard typically involves putting in sustained and focused labour towards your goals. To get rich, you have to work hard on:
- Skill Development
- Persistence
- Entrepreneurship
- Investing your Time and Energy
- Constant Learning
- Smart Decision-Making
- Establishing Good Networking.

Along with hard work you need financial literacy, strategic thinking, and the capacity to seize opportunity and convert it into success.

Hard work and prosperity go hand in hand. They are two sides of the same coin. Just as a strong foundation supports a grand structure, similarly diligent efforts provide the foundation for achieving financial freedom. Some of the benefits of hard work are listed below:

- **Skills Hard:** Work can help you polish skills and acquire newer skills. Continuous practice and learning leads to expertise, which opens up the door to better gains and opportunities.
- **Efforts Compound:** Small incremental steps accumulate into significant benefits and gradual outcomes that lead to big gains.
- **Delayed Gratification:** Hard work results into delayed gratifications, that is, letting go of immediate small benefits for a larger benefit. At times, what is good now may not be good in future and might even be a disaster later. Hard work stops us from getting lured by immediate and short-term benefits. Often, immediate rewards are traps that yield poor outcome in future. Delayed rewards tend to build wealth over the time.
- **Resilience:** There will be many obstacles, setbacks, and challenges during our journey towards our financial goals. Hard work will help us find solutions to the problems, rather than complain about them. It teaches us to adapt and pursue our goals rather than giving up in the face of adversities.
- **Reputation:** Expertise, resilience and perseverance leads to strong credibility. People will have a positive outlook about you and your reliability.

- **Networking:** Good reputation builds trust in the eyes of others and lays foundation for building strong associations and networks. It attracts other reputed individuals who share same work ethics, leading to strong partnerships in business and society. Strong and reliable association will enhance your problem-solving skills and help you reach larger audience and market.

Hard work is not just about slogging mindlessly over long working hours. It is about continuous efforts, constant learning and resilience. It is about strong commitment towards success of your financial goals.

Remember, there are no shortcuts to success. Hard work is the cornerstone of wealth, the foundation upon which prosperity is built. It transforms dreams into reality, turning aspirations into fortunes. The path to riches is paved with the dedication to toil tirelessly, for the crucible of effort, success is forged.

Doctrine 39

Don't Overspend, But Don't Cut Off Small Pleasures

THE WEALTH JOURNEY teaches you to control your expenses. If you want to save money for your future, you cannot spend extravagantly today. However, this does not mean that you should not spend on small pleasures like eating out, or hanging out with friends and family. Cutting down small expenses will not make you rich, but it will definitely make you feel deprived and unhappy.

Decent clothes, self-grooming, entertainment—these are the small pleasures of life and you should enjoy them. Spending money on these will make you feel good and will also help you to achieve your financial goals.

You can complain about unnecessary expenses, you can work out on managing leaks, you can be tight fisted, but you should not compromise on small pleasures. Maintain a firm check on your budget, but make sure to have a provision for the small pleasures of your life.

If you cannot afford, buy less, but don't deprive yourself. Rather, treat yourself. Experience little luxuries.

If you don't experience the good things of life then how will you crave for it; if you don't crave then how can you aspire for it. If you don't aspire then how can you desire to create wealth? These small pleasures are the elixirs for a wealthy life.

Wealthy people don't scrimp and save. Some of them are very tight fisted but they do spend on small pleasures of life.

Little indulgences of luxury will help you run after money. Stay committed towards your goal of wealth creation, preservation and transfer. Living and enjoying the present moment shifts your focus from worrying about the future or dwelling on the past remorse. Shift your focus to appreciate what you have, and express your gratitude towards life and people. This will lead you to a more meaningful and content life.

True wealth lies not only in accumulating riches but also in savouring the small pleasures of life. Enjoy it.

In addition to balancing your spending, it's crucial to live in the moment and enjoy the present. Life is not just about the future; it's about the here and now. Embracing the present moment allows you to appreciate the small joys that life offers daily. Whether it's a beautiful sunset, a good meal, or a laugh with friends, these moments make life rich and fulfilling.

By enjoying the present, you create a balanced approach to wealth that includes financial security and personal fulfilment.

Remember, the journey to wealth is not just about accumulating money but also about enjoying the process and the small pleasures along the way. So, while you save and invest for the future, don't forget to live in the moment and cherish the present.

Living in the moment and savouring experiences can create lasting memories that enrich our lives in ways beyond the momentary satisfaction of material possessions. When we spend on experiences—like travelling, attending events, or simply enjoying a meal with loved ones—we engage our senses and emotions, creating vivid and meaningful memories cherishable for years. These experiences often bring more happiness and fulfilment than material items which lose their novelty and appeal over time. Unlike instant gratification from buying things, experiences foster connections, personal growth, and a deeper appreciation for life.

Here are some examples of living in the moment:

- **Mindful Eating**: Take time to savour each bite from your meal; appreciate the flavours, textures, and aromas. This practice not only enhances your dining experience but also promotes better digestion and mindfulness.
- **Nature Walks**: Spend time in nature, whether it's a walk in the park, a hike in the mountains, or a stroll along the beach. Pay attention to the sights, sounds, and smells around you, and let yourself be fully present in the experience.
- **Quality Time with Loved Ones**: Engage in meaningful conversations and activities with family and friends. Put away your phone and other distractions to actively connect and enjoy each other's company.
- **Creative Activities**: Engage in hobbies like painting, writing, or playing a musical instrument. These activities can help you express yourself and immerse in the present moment.

- **Meditation and Deep Breathing**: Practice meditation or deep breathing exercises to centre yourself and focus on the present. These practices can help calm your mind and reduce stress.
- **Gratitude Journaling**: Keep a journal where you write down things you are grateful for every day. This practice helps you focus on the positive aspects of your life and appreciate the present moment.

One of my most cherished practices is to deeply thank my father, grandfather, and other family members for leaving me a legacy of good deeds, practices, and values. This profound inheritance has instilled in me a sense of trusteeship over wealth, guiding me to view it not as an owner but as a steward entrusted with the responsibility to manage and nurture it for the greater good.

Remember, the idea is to enjoy the little pleasures of life without going overboard on expenses. This will fill you with an unmatched contentment and fulfilment, without compromising on your goal of wealth creation.

Doctrine 40

Investment Is A Difficult Art

WHILE WRITING THIS book, I got the news of the sad demise of the great investor, Charlie Munger. His investing lessons flooded my mind and so I thought to dedicate this doctrine to him out of respect.

There were many words of wisdom he had shared through his life experience as an investor. As a tribute to him, I am noting down some of the pointers here. Try to read these pointers again and again and follow them throughout your journey of wealth creation:

- If investing wasn't hard, everyone would be rich.
- In the wealth creation journey, remember you don't have to be brilliant, only a little bit wiser than the others, on average, for a long time.
- It's waiting that helps you as an investor but a lot of people just can't wait.
- You need patience, discipline, and agility to take losses and adversities without going crazy.

- Live with your income and save so you can invest. Learn what you need to learn.
- Money to be made in the stock market is not through the buying or the selling, but in the waiting.
- Great opportunities are rare. So we should grab whenever we come across.
- He mentioned once that he wanted to be rich not to buy a Ferrari but to achieve financial freedom.
- Investing is where you find great companies and then sit on your ass.
- Keep things simple.
- The desire to get rich fast is pretty dangerous.
- Those who keep learning will keep rising in life.
- A lot of people with high IQs are terrible investors because they have terrible temperaments.
- Knowing what you don't know is more useful than being brilliant.
- Passion is more important than brainpower.
- Develop into a lifelong self-learner through voracious reading; cultivate curiosity and strive to become a little wiser every day.
- Understand the human psychology in investing. Recognising common cognitive biases and emotional pitfalls can help make more rational decisions.
- Savings are essential for a sane and happy life.
- The rule for a happy life is low expectations.
- The first rule is not to lose. The second rule is not to forget the first rule.

There are various learnings from Charlie Munger. What I have learnt from Warren Buffett and Charlie Munger is to understand the basics of savings and investing.

The famous quote of Warren Buffett says it all, 'If you want to invest, first learn to save.' This is a basic and golden rule to create wealth.

The essence of this advice underscores the importance of building a foundation of financial discipline and saving before venturing into investments.

Before you start allocating funds to various investment opportunities, it is crucial to develop a habit of systematic money saving. Savings provide financial confidence, and ensure security and the capital needed to grab the investment opportunities.

Savings helps you to accumulate the necessary funds for future investments without relying on debt.

This principle helps you to establish a solid financial base through saving before delving into the potentially rewarding, but complex, world of investing.

In conclusion, understand this basic idea with the help of a metaphor—a rupee saved is a seed planted; through careful nurturing, it grows into the tree of a financial security. Investing is the sunlight that transforms those savings into the fruits of wealth.

Doctrine 41

Working For Others Will Not Make You Rich

MANY ENTREPRENEURS AND financial advisors advise that working for others does not make you rich, but it is not necessarily true. This ideology says that if you depend on only one source of income then your journey of financial independence may take time or it may be difficult.

If you have good skills in your domain then you can earn a good salary and climb the corporate ladder fast enough to earn a fortune. It all depends on how you sharpen your skillset. Along with your employment you can work on cultivating entrepreneurship skills that will create multiple income sources for you.

If we look around, we may find many individuals who have created wealth with steady employment and careful investment planning. So it is not true that if you want to be rich, you have to work for yourself and not for others. There are many CEOs and higher post-bearers in employment who are rich.

The key to financial freedom is to understand your individual goals, explore the various avenues and to make informed decisions based on personal circumstances and aspirations. If you are working for others, your first priority should be ensuring the stability of employment. The second priority should be to develop other sources of income from hobbies or skills and focusing on savings and systematic investments.

Many of my acquaintances are working as IT Experts, engineers, skilled professionals, and designers among others, and they are doing quite well. Corporate companies need knowledgeable professionals and when you have good knowledge and expertise of your domain, then they will pay you well with additional perks and facilities.

You also need to understand that working for others might not always make you rich. We all have our individual capabilities, aspirations and financial circumstances based on which we have to make our career decisions. We all know that the majority of startups struggled and ended up in closures too. When you have your own startups, you have to face the field-specific challenges.

Time has changed and in today's corporate world there are many opportunities which might be better than your small business or startup.

So, remember, whether you work for others or for yourself, you can always excel based on your individual temperament, knowledge and planning. Either ways, you have to look for multiple income streams; you have to save and invest and follow all the doctrines discussed in this book to create wealth. So keep walking ahead.

Doctrine 42

Act And Excel, Delay And Doom

MONEY DECISIONS HAVE to be quick. You have to act timely, if you fail to act, you lose an opportunity. It might sound odd, but many investors have lost opportunities just by not being able to make a decision. Many a times we keep our money idle in a savings account, while losing out on many good investment opportunities.

Once you have decided on your goals and investment strategies, then you have to act. However, the decision-making process is based on various factors like your risk appetite, your nature, circumstances, fear, doubts, advice and many more. So you have to train yourself to take well-balanced, informed decisions based on your goals, strategy and financial acumen. Although the doctrines discussed in this book will help you to prepare yourself for making quick decisions, at the same time you have to work on your nature and habits. Many of us have a tendency to procrastinate almost everything. So you have to work on that carefully.

Doing something is always better than doing nothing. And acting fast can be better than holding. Throughout my professional journey, I have observed that most of the successful investors have the unique trait of making quick decisions. This can be achieved with a clarity in financial goals and financial literacy.

To create wealth by making fast decisions you need a combination of skills and strategies. Let's look at some of the prerequisites to acquire this skill:

- **Information Synthesis:** Develop a habit to collect all possible data or information quickly and synthesise the relevant information. Always stay informed about market trends and news to explore potential opportunities.
- **Risk Assessment:** Master the skill of risk assessment. You should know the possible downside of your decisions and weigh them against potential gains. You have to develop your analytical thinking to achieve this.
- **Decision Flow Chart:** Create a decision-making framework that aligns with your financial goals. Define criteria that help you to rapidly evaluate options considering factors like ROI, market conditions and long-term viability.
- **Adaptability:** You should know how to adjust and time your strategy swiftly based on new information or in the face of unexpected events.
- **Emotions Control:** You should learn how to control emotions like fear and greed to make your decisions quick. This will help you to prevent making impulsive decisions.
- **Networking :** Build a strong network of trusted advisors and mentors. Consult experts in relevant fields to gain insights that help you to make fast decisions.

- **Continuous Learning:** Financial landscapes evolve and are hence dynamic. So continuous learning is essential. Keep yourself well informed by reading, discussing, and attending seminars.
- **Automation:** Implement systems and processes that automate routine decisions. This allows you to focus on more critical and essential areas and will give you time to enhance your knowledge by reading and other activities as discussed.
- **Scenario Planning:** We will discuss this later in the book; this is called 'What If' situation. Anticipate the potential outcome of decisions and have a contingency plan in place.

The proactive approach minimises the impact of unforeseen events.
- **Decisiveness:** Practice divisiveness. Avoid procrastination and analysis paralysis. Trust your instincts supported by your knowledge, experiences and circumstances, to make decisions promptly.

Lastly, understand that the prerequisite is not just the speed, but the combination of speed and accuracy. Fast decisions can be powerful, but they need to be well informed so that they align with your long-term wealth creation goals. Coincidentally, while writing this, I am watching a T20 match between India and Australia, where the Indian team has attempted scoring fast runs but without a well thought out plan and strategy and so they have started losing wickets rapidly. This further underlines the importance of making a quick but prudent decision.

To conclude, wise decisions made in time are always better than unorganised decisions made in haste. Think on your feet but do not trade-off prudence.

Doctrine 43

Don't Run After Money

WE WORK BECAUSE we need money. Some of us work because it is their passion. Some look at work as an activity; they are well-off so they don't need money hence they choose to take up work as an activity.

When you work for money, without showing your need you get an upper hand. People tend to exploit when they know someone is working for money.

One of my acquaintances had a good business. However, he didn't like the kind of work he was doing. What happened because of this? A good running business eventually failed. This brings home the point that you have to follow your passion and not money. I, too, decided to write books because writing is my passion. Even though I might not write well, I continued the practice without anticipating publishing it. And now you have my book in your hand. So running after money will not get you results but running after passion might.

This is the secret behind the success of the rich. They

follow their passion and try to know everything about the field of their passion. They leave no gaps in their knowledge. The wealthy people know where they are going and what they will do once they reach there. They have passion, drive, ambition and determination. They work because they like it and they want to.

Passion and determination is vital for success. These are the two traits that you can develop and emulate from the life of a rich person. You have to do like them to become like them. You have to work as if you don't need money.

Chasing money without purpose can lead to unfulfilling pursuits. Instead, focus on personal growth, passion and drive endeavours. Try to provide value to others. By working on your skills and goals and contributing positively to the world, you may find money as a by-product of your efforts. Many of us may not be liking our current work but are continuing it for their livelihood and family. Look at it as a medium to build capital for your passion and hobby. It will help you enjoy what you are doing and keep you focused towards your goal.

In a nutshell, don't run after money; chase purpose, cultivate passion, and let wealth follow as a reflection of your meaningful pursuits.

Doctrine 44

Sharpen Your Skills

IDENTIFY THE ONE skill which you excel in. Narrow down on your micro-niche. Work on that micro-niche and sharpen your skills.

Know about everything possible in that micro-niche and learn it thoroughly. Once you sharpen your micro-niche, go and tell the world about it. Make optimum use of PR. Create social media accounts on platforms like Facebook, Instagram, LinkedIn, and YouTube among others. Maintain a good website. Try to solve problems of people while working in your micro-niche. You will notice a remarkable difference in the results.

Once you develop a mastery in your micro-niche, you can do something no one else can, or maybe only a few can. At this stage, you have made your name and so you can demand your price.

The world is hungry for new things and new skills. When you master your micro-niche, you teach the world those skills.

By doing this, you are solving the problem of many people and that's why you can demand your price and become rich. Remember, your micro-niche need not be a difficult one, just one that the world wants to learn and is ready to pay for, for example, a guitar course for CEOs.

Know your strengths and weaknesses. Find out your passion. Understand your talents and skills. How can you put those skills and talents to the best use? Next, find out who wants to learn that skill? Once you know this, you have to focus on marketing your skills so that people come to know of it. If you can design a full-length course on your skills, then you can put it on a digital platform and have your LMS (Learning Management System) platform. By doing this you can market your course systematically. You can have:

- Your website
- Your LMS system
- Your social media handles like Facebook, Instagram, LinkedIn, YouTube channel
- Your marketing funnel

You can earn through digital platforms and master your skills to become a mentor, consultant, or a coach.

You should have trust in yourself and your skills, patience to market your course and sharpen your skills and to create your name or brand.

As Warren Buffett wisely said, 'The more you learn, the more you earn.'

Cultivating or sharpening a skill is often linked to wealth for several reasons. First, having a valuable skill makes you an asset in the job market or as an entrepreneur. High demand skills can lead to better job opportunities.

Additionally, continuous skill development keeps you adaptable in a changing economy. This ability to learn and apply new skills enables you to thrive in evolving industries and enhances your long-term earning potential.

Mastering a skill involves gaining expertise over time, which can lead to increased efficiency and productivity. This efficiency can make you rich, especially if you are self-employed or working in roles where the output directly correlates with earnings.

When you sharpen your skill, you invest in yourself, increasing your value and marketability which can significantly contribute to achieving financial success and wealth over time.

In conclusion, cultivating skills is the key to unlocking the door of wealth. Each skill acquired is a strategic investment in your financial success. Make sure you make the most of it.

Doctrine 45

Earn A Living Versus Making Money

WE ALL WORK for our living. We need money for our daily life needs. We need money for ourselves and our family. While earning for our living, we get so busy that we hardly get time to earn extra or to explore ways and means to earn more money to get rich and achieve our dream goal—living an FFL, Financial Freedom Lifestyle.

Our routine job and its related activities eat up most of our time. We get so busy with the routine that we forget our end goal—to earn more money.

Remember that to create wealth you have to think beyond the 9 am to 5 pm routine work or the activities that consume most of your time and energy.

The harsh truth is that the majority spend their whole life earning a living and so they fail to think beyond this. On the other hand, the rich go beyond this and get the time to indulge in the activities that get them more money.

If you work for a living completely knowing that it will

not make you rich, then you must be continuing it because you love it.

If you love what you do then the amount you earn doesn't matter to you. It is good that you are enjoying by following your passion but if you want to earn wealth then you need to plan where you will earn more money from. You need to ensure that your passion doesn't keep you occupied for long. If you don't get the time for other pursuits to earn money, then your wealth creation will be in problem.

If you are not happy with either the work you are doing or the pay you are getting then you should ask yourself why are you still doing that? Most of the time people don't like their job/pay but still they continue as it is their only means of earning a living.

So, don't get too busy in earning your living that you do not get any time to create wealth. Find yourself time and energy to earn better.

Remember, you have to hold your head high and look for all the possible opportunities around and seize them. Essentially, the pursuit of a living becomes so consuming that it hinders the pursuit of additional financial growth.

Doctrine 46

Saving Small Or Saving Big?

LET'S LOOK AT the debate between two popular investment strategies—one coming into the limelight recently, and another a staple for centuries.

Systematic Investment Plans (SIPs): Small Is Powerful
Let's start by examining **Systematic Investment Plans (SIPs)**, which have become very popular recently and are often accompanied with the adage 'Small Is Powerful'. The core idea of SIPs is to invest small, fixed amount at regular intervals, which over time, snowballs into a substantial sum of money. It is not a new concept, and is similar to the lessons learnt from childhood stories about the thirsty crow or the ant and the grasshopper. It emphasises the value of discipline and consistent efforts leading to significant results.

SIPs are not exclusive to mutual funds. The same principles apply to life insurance premiums, Employee Provident Fund (EPF), Public Provident Fund (PPF), National Pension System (NPS) contributions, and recurring deposits. Even home loans operate on this principle, where Equated Monthly Instalments (EMIs) allow the borrowers to repay large sums over time. The key to the success of these small, regular contributions is that they foster discipline and patience—virtues essential for financial growth.

But, does this mean that small, regular contributions are the best way to build wealth because they encourage discipline and patience? Let's explore other options too.

Real Estate Investments: The Power of Large, One-Time Investments
There are numerous examples where a relatively small initial investment in property has yielded substantial gains over the years, benefiting especially the next generation. This has led to the common belief that investing in real estate is one of the surest ways to become rich and wealthy as there are countless instances where modest sums have grown into crores.

The key factor behind such impressive returns is the significant amount of money initially invested in real estate. Real estate investments typically require large sums of money and a long holding period. Even with modest or average returns, the sheer size of the initial investment and the extended time frame can result in substantial growth.

Example Comparison: SIPs vs Real Estate
To illustrate this, let's look at some data from the FundsIndia Wealth Conversation Report (August 2024):
- **Nifty 50 TRI**: Delivered a Compound Annual Growth Rate (CAGR) of 16.10 per cent, multiplying investments by 19.7 times.

- **Real Estate:** Delivered a CAGR of 8.40 per cent, multiplying investments by 5 times.

  Here's a practical example:
- **SIP in Nifty 50 TRI:** A Rs 5,000 monthly SIP over 20 years would grow to approximately Rs 86,32,000.
- **Real Estate Investment:** A one-time investment of Rs 25,00,000 in real estate over the same period would grow to around Rs 1,25,00,000.

This example demonstrates that while small regular contributions can build significant wealth through disciplined investing, a large one-time contribution can also generate substantial returns over an extended period.

The Importance of Compound Interest in Wealth Building

To clearly understand the difference between saving small amounts regularly and saving large amounts occasionally, let's examine the compound interest formula:

$$A = P(1+NR)^{nt}$$

- **A** = the amount of money accumulated after years, including interest.
- **P** = the principal amount (initial investment).
- **R** = annual interest rate (decimal).
- **N** = number of times interest is compounded per year.
- **T** = time the money is invested for in years.

The total amount of money after the compounding period (A) is determined by all four components working together, not by any single component. Often, we fail at compounding money because we focus only on one component, such as the rate of return (R). Even if we achieve a higher rate of return, if the time period (t) is very short—just days or months—the final value and gain will not be significant. Similarly, even if the principal amount (P) is large, without sufficient time, the outcome will still be limited.

For substantial wealth accumulation, all components—principal, rate of return, compounding frequency, and time—need to work in harmony. This holistic approach ensures that the power of compound interest is fully realised, leading to meaningful and substantial financial growth.

Synopsis: The Importance of Early and Consistent Savings
Starting your career with small, regular contributions is crucial. It helps you develop the habit of saving early on. If you wait for a higher income to start saving, you might find it challenging to begin even after earning more than required. Learning to build financial discipline with low income is essential as higher income often increases distractions. Once your income increases, you can supplement your regular contributions with occasional larger savings to reap the benefits of compounding. This balanced approach ensures steady financial growth and monetary accumulation over time.

The Final Twist: Converting Savings into Investments
Saving is important, whether it be small and regular amounts or large and occasional amounts. The key to building wealth lies in converting those savings into investments. Savings help you generate post-tax returns that match the inflation rate, while investments allow you to outperform inflation with a reasonable margin.

The key takeaways from this doctrine would be to focus on getting real returns, that is, returns after accounting for taxes and inflation, rather than aiming for the maximum return. Add to your principal consistently and maintain a long investment horizon to maximise your financial growth. This strategy will help you build substantial wealth over time.

Doctrine 47

Stick To Your Wealth Creation Plan

ONCE YOU HAVE identified your long-term goals and have made a plan to achieve it, then stick to it without fail.

Once you prepare a strategy, don't meddle with it. Revising it repeatedly will not improve it, rather you may spoil it. Don't fiddle and flip. It stands true for all strategies. The more you think, the more changes you will consider.

Not fiddling with the wealth creation plan means avoiding frequent and impulsive changes to the investment strategy. It suggests maintaining a long-term perspective, resisting the urge to react to short-term market fluctuations, and sticking to the carefully-crafted financial plan. This approach helps minimise unnecessary risks and allows compounding to work in your favour over time. Regularly reassess and adjust your plan if needed, but avoid constant tinkering based on short-term market movements. Consistency and discipline often lead to more successful wealth creation.

Your plan needs time to nurture. You must have the patience

to execute it effectively. Remember, your plan is for the long-term, so any short-term turbulence should not disturb you.

You should track the market and its trends but don't change your investment strategy. Keep doing your homework, keep learning but without changing your investment strategy as new changes will ruin your long-term perspective.

Maintaining a consistent investment strategy aligns with long-term financial goals, thereby reducing emotional decision-making. Frequent changes also lead to increased transaction costs, including brokerage fees and taxes.

Many examples show that long-term investors who follow a well-defined strategy tend to fare better than those who frequently change their approach based on short-term market fluctuations.

Regularly reassessing and adjusting your strategy based on significant life changes or shifts in financial goals is advisable, but impulsive changes can be counterproductive.

Successful investing is about managing risks. Stay disciplined, stick to your strategy, and remember the wise words of Warren Buffett, 'The stock market is designed to transfer money from the active to the patient.'

Remember, this is applicable not only to investments; it is equally applicable to our vocation, job, profession, business, and skills among others. How many have benefited from frequent change in job, business, skill, hobby etc.? Take your time to decide, but once decided give it your time, monitor it and make refinements, if required, but stop finding newer and better ways. Whether it be money, work or relationship, you need to give time and keep at it with a steady pace.

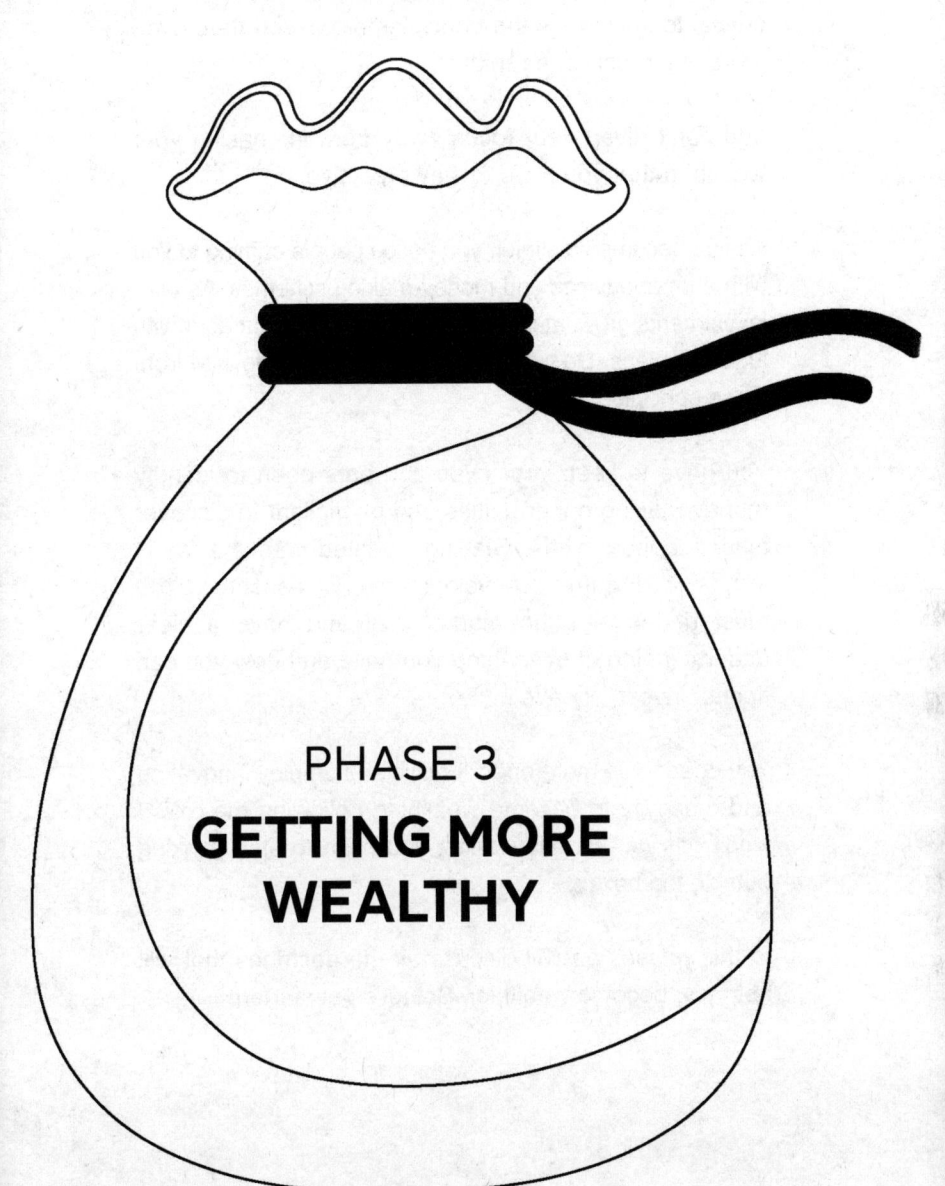

Once you have accumulated some wealth, the scenario changes. Money begets money; the more money you have, the more it can grow. You can't sit back and enjoy what you've acquired. Wealth can disappear quickly if kept idle. Now that you've gained some wealth, it's crucial to implement the principles discussed here even more vigorously and rapidly.

You can't divert your focus away from increasing your wealth; rather you have to stay proactive.

As you become wealthier, you notice people coming to you with a lot of advices and money-making schemes. As your investments grow, many advisors appear on your door with lucrative plans. Do listen to them, but do not deviate from these principles.

You have to keep your eyes and ears open to identify money-making opportunities and be vigilant to discover hidden opportunities. Staying updated with the latest trends and current developments is essential. You must understand the market well and have a clear understanding of everything you have and how you can spend, invest, or save it.

You need to be more opportunistic and employ innovation and creativity to become wealthier. Following the crowd won't get you serious wealth; you have to start thinking outside the box.

In this phase, we will discuss all the doctrines that will help you become wealthier. So, let's get started!

Doctrine 48

Financial Health Check-Up

TO INCREASE YOUR prosperity, you need to maintain a healthy awareness of your current financial standing. You can do this on a monthly or quarterly basis, but it has to be done at fixed regular intervals.

For the financial health check-up, you can consider the following steps or customise your own check-up plan:

- **Budget Review:** Check your income to expense ratio. Ensure you are spending less than you earn.
- **Savings and Emergency Fund:** You should have a minimum of six months' worth of living expenses saved.
- **Debt Assessment:** Review your outstanding debts, credit card balances, and loans. Make sure you pay back high-interest debts, as discussed in the previous doctrines.
- **Investment Portfolio:** Evaluate your financial portfolio to ensure it aligns with your financial goals and risk tolerance.
- **Retirement Planning:** Assess your retirement savings and compare it to your retirement goals. Consider increasing

contributions, if necessary.
- **Insurance Coverage:** Review all your insurance policies, such as health, life, auto, and home among others to ensure you have adequate coverage.
- **Credit Score:** Check and manage your credit score if it is not healthy.
- **Financial Goals:** Keep checking and updating your financial goals on a regular basis. What are you saving for, and are you on the right track to achieve your goals?
- **Tax Planning:** Optimise your tax strategy to minimise your tax liability.
- **Estate Planning:** Ensure your will, power of attorney, and other estate planning documents are up to date.
- **Professional Help:** Consider consulting a financial expert for a comprehensive assessment.

The above points are for reference only; do your homework and make a check list to be reviewed at regular intervals. You can refer to *The Checklist Manifesto: How to Get Things Right* by Atul Gawande, which explores the power of checklists in improving outcomes across various fields. The author distinguishes between errors of ignorance (lack of knowledge) and errors of ineptitude (not applying what we know). The latter is a more common cause of mistakes by even the most competent professionals. It covers how the use of checklists has transformed medicine, disaster response, investment banking, business and other domains.

Regular financial health check-ups can help you make informed decisions to improve your financial well-being.

Conducting a financial health check-up regularly will give

you a pulse on your financial well-being. It will help you:
- Act quickly in response to different financial changes.
- Maintain better focus.
- Make well-informed decisions.
- Act timely to seize various opportunities. Prevent various financial leakages.
- Boost your confidence, enabling you to take calculated risks.
- Regular financial health check-ups serve as a compass that guides you toward your financial goals and keeps you on the path of financial well-being.

In a nutshell, knowing your current financial standing will help you make better and more informed financial decisions. Be it your investment plans, savings, or budgeting, a financial health check-up is indispensable.

Doctrine 49

Money Mentor

A MENTOR IS a person who can support, advice, and guide you. The concept of mentorship has been around since the time of Socrates and is useful for every walk of life. Mentorship is imperative for personal development, career, and wealth creation. Many successful businessmen, celebrities, and wealthy individuals have mentors, and sometimes even more than one.

A mentor can be instrumental in wealth creation for several reasons:

- **Knowledge and Experience:** Mentors have years of experience and knowledge in their field. Based on their expertise and exposure, they can provide valuable insights, guidance, and advice, having learnt from their own successes and failures, thereby helping you avoid mistakes.
- **Clarity of Goals and Execution:** Mentors can present ideas clearly and concisely, facilitating goal setting and execution.
- **Networking Opportunities:** Mentors can introduce you to valuable connections and networks that can open doors to various investment opportunities.

- **Emotional and Moral Support:** Building wealth is a challenging journey, and mentors provide valuable support, motivation, and encouragement during tough times.
- **Learning from Mistakes:** Mentors can help you learn from your past financial mistakes, helping you avoid costly errors in the future.
- **Personalised and Professional Advice:** Since mentors are independent and without vested interests, they can provide tailor-made advice based on your financial situation and goals.
- **Confidence and Future Perspective:** Mentors are available to address your queries and doubts, boosting your confidence in your abilities. They can also clarify your future investment perspective.

'The best mentors can help us define and express our inner calling.'—Anthony Tjan

Choosing the right financial mentor is a real challenge. You should be specific about your requirements when seeking a financial mentor and ask yourself questions such as:
- What kind of mentor suits my needs?
- Where and how can I find them?
- What will be the fees?
- How can I utilise their abilities to the fullest?

Your financial mentor should have your best interests in mind and help you make the right decisions at the right time. Before choosing your financial mentor, check the following:
- Experience and Credentials.
- References, Recommendations, and Past Track Records.

- Compatibility with your Nature, Risk Appetite, and Financial Conditions.
- Commitment and Availability.
- Transparency, Trust, and Goodwill.
- Clarity on Terms and Conditions.
- Your Instinct

Your money mentor should be financially successful, as this demonstrates their abilities. If your mentor has successfully managed their own finances, you can have confidence in them. Remember the following quote when choosing your mentor, 'Money Mentors are people who have proved their financial acumen by making a bit of money themselves.'

Money mentors are there for advice, information, suggestions, restraint, support, and encouragement. If you choose them well and use their guidance effectively, your wealth creation is assured. So, start your search for a suitable money mentor.

We can conclude that when choosing a money mentor, it's crucial to find someone who is flexible and committed to continuous learning, while maintaining steadfast core principles and ideology. Money is dynamic; being too rigid can be counterproductive. However, money can also be elusive and tempting; being too fluid can also be detrimental. There needs to be a balance—have strong roots to stay grounded and reach new heights, and a flexible trunk to withstand strong winds.

Doctrine 50

Intuition

'LISTEN TO YOUR heart', 'follow your gut feeling', 'I knew this was going to happen', 'believe in your intuition,' these are the kinds of phrases we often hear and read.

Intuition can indeed play a role in wealth building, but it should be used in conjunction with rational financial planning and decision-making. Using your intuition in wealth building is an art that can be learned through practice. Here is a simple flow chart on using your intuition in financial planning:

- Listen to your intuition.
- Do your research to find out if your intuition is worth following.
- Based on your intuition, create a plan and consult your money mentor.
- Listen to and act according to your money mentor's advice.

Many wealthy people have made money based on their intuition. You should be able to capture that magic moment of intuition and turn it into an execution plan for success.

Let's dive deeper to understand how intuition helps create wealth:

- **Gut Feeling for Opportunities:**
  Intuition can help you identify investment opportunities that may not be immediately apparent through data or analysis. Trusting your intuition can lead you to explore hidden opportunities that could be profitable. It requires a lot of practice and learning but can be learned and implemented by anyone willing to approach it with patience and gradual pace.
- **Timing Decisions:**
  Intuition can assist in timing financial decisions, such as buying or selling assets or shares. An intuition-based sense of timing can be very helpful in timely investment moves.
- **Risk Assessments:**
  Intuition can work as an alarm for potential risks. If something doesn't feel right about a financial decision, it's worth investigating further to ensure there are no hidden risks.
- **Emotional Risk Management:**
  Intuition can help you gauge your emotional state when making financial choices. However, you have to balance intuition with financial knowledge, risk analysis, and expert advice, as explained earlier.

Understand risk management and the role of intuition with the following metaphor—intuition in financial management is the whisper of wisdom amid the noise of numbers, guiding you towards informed decisions and prosperous outcomes.

Word of Caution: Well practiced intuition will certainly have benefits, but don't be impatient for the outcome. It takes time and tests our patience. Sometimes, it may not even work; your intuition is not a guideline for the world as to how it will act and react. Accept everything with grace and find learning opportunities. Every adversity holds a lesson not visible with arrogance or complaints but only with grace.

Doctrine 51

Strike, Attack!

YOU HAVE TO be more proactive after you have created some wealth. When we have a bit of money, there is a temptation to sit back, relax, and enjoy the wealth. But remember that now is the time to attack and strike to create more wealth. Now is the time to capitalise and consolidate your wealth. Look for more opportunities to invest. Invest in stocks or real estate, start a new business, or look for hidden assets and opportunities.

If you plan efficiently at this stage, you can achieve the FFL. You have to double your efforts, refresh your enthusiasm, ignite the fire within you, and attack! You should not sit back. The wealthy never take a break; they work harder and enjoy the great rewards.

You have to keep doing whatever made you rich. Ride on your success stride and explore more. If you have found any success formula, try and find more. Keep learning, exploring, and experimenting. Don't ever think that you know it all. Keep working harder than everyone around you.

Now is the time to hire money mentors and elevate yourself from an amateur investor to a pro. Remember every detail of your journey and follow it again. Revise your goals and work towards achieving them.

This is where most people fail as they think they have achieved everything and they remain happy with what they have. But observe the rich around you. What do they do? Are they sitting idle with the bit of wealth they have, or are they working harder trying to build up on their wealth?

What do the rich people do when they have some wealth? They:

- **Invest more:**
  They invest in stocks, bonds, real estate, or startups to potentially generate more wealth over time.
- **Philanthropy:**
  They establish foundations or donate to causes they care about. They engage in charitable giving as they believe in giving back. When you give back, you keep getting both wealth and satisfaction.
- **Business Ventures:**
  They start new ventures or invest in existing ones to expand their entrepreneurial endeavours.
- **Estate Planning:**
  Wealthy people often engage in estate planning to ensure their wealth is passed on to their heirs.
- **Tax Planning:**
  They plan their taxes to minimise their tax liabilities legally.
- **Diversification:**
  The wealthy diversify their investments to spread risk and protect their wealth.

- **Live Financial Freedom Lifestyle:**
  They start pursuing their hobbies and passions and enjoy the FFL life.
- **Education and Self-Improvement:**
  They invest in new learning and skills development to maintain their wealth.

The choices individuals make with their wealth can vary widely based on their values, priorities, and financial goals. So, be prepared to strike and attack to get more wealth.

Doctrine 52

Delegate

DELEGATING EFFECTIVELY IS an important skill in creating and managing wealth. It allows one to focus on higher value tasks while entrusting various responsibilities to others. This can increase your productivity and help you leverage the skills and expertise of others to grow your wealth.

Many business people hire money mentors because of the many financial things they know nothing about. Similarly, there is a lot of other work which we don't know much about and learning them gets time-consuming. So the best way out in such a scenario is to delegate those works to experts. Do what you are good at, and get others to do the things you can't. It is simple—pick really good people and let them work for you to make you wealthy.

Let's see how delegating tasks can work for you in creating wealth:

- **Focus on high value tasks:**
  By delegating routine or time-consuming tasks to others,

you can focus on high value activities such as strategic planning, decision-making, and exploring new income generating opportunities.

- **Leverage Expertise:**
Delegating allows you to tap into the expertise and skills of others. You can delegate tasks to experts and thereby improve the quality and efficiency of those tasks.
- **Scalability:**
Delegation can help you to scale up your efforts for creating wealth. As you expand your business or investment portfolio, you can't handle everything on your own. Delegating allows your wealth creation to grow without being limited by your personal capacity.
- **Risk Management:**
Delegating can also help mitigate risk. When you rely on the expertise of others in areas like financial management, legal matters, or market analysis, you reduce the chance of making costly mistakes.
- **Time Efficiency:**
Time is a valuable resource and effective delegation can save your time. The saved time can be used for focusing on wealth creation, personal growth, networking and other activities.
- **Diversification:**
Delegating can extend to investment strategies. Diversifying your investments across different asset classes or industries can be a form of delegation to experts in those fields, spreading risk and potentially increasing your wealth.

Successful delegation requires clear communication, trust and the ability to oversee and manage the tasks delegated. It is a skill that can enhance your wealth building efforts.

Follow some of these tips to delegate your work effectively:
- Identify which type of work you should delegate as every work might not be suitable for delegating.
- You have to inculcate the ability to let it go to delegate as without this you can't delegate. Don't confuse dictate with delegate. There is a thin line between the both, so mind your mind.
- Delegate as per your priorities.
- Understand the person's strength to whom you are delegating.
- Care for the person whom you are delegating.
- Keep the person well informed and train him properly.
- Praise and motivate them.
- Set realistic targets.
- Set a good example as they will love to work for the person whom they admire.
- Maintain distance, dignity and authority with the people whom you delegate.

To conclude, delegation is an art that you can learn as you go. If you master this art it will be very helpful for wealth creation as well as wealth preservation.

Doctrine 53

Are You A Solopreneur Or A Team Player?

ASK YOURSELF SOME pertinent questions:
- Am I good on my own or do I need others?
- Should I build a team and act as a team player?
- Can I work well with partner/s?
- Do I know my strengths and weaknesses well?
- Do I know what I am good or bad at?

We all have our peculiarities of nature. I myself feel that I am at my best when working alone for some of the tasks, but for others I need a helping hand. If you know your work tendencies well then you can plan accordingly.

You have to work on your strengths so that you can trade it off well. For your weaknesses, identify people who can compensate and help you overcome those.

As far as the partner/s are concerned, you should team up with those who are expert in diverse fields and not limited to similar niche. Having a same set of expertise, skill, and strength and weakness can create conflict.

Determining whether you are more suited to being a solopreneur or a team player depends on your personal preferences, strengths and working style:

- **Working Style:**
  - Solopreneur: If you prefer working independently, making decision on your own and controlling everything, then you are a solopreneur.
  - Team Player: If you enjoy collaborating with others, sharing responsibilities and working together to achieve common goals, then you are a team player.
- **Skills and Expertise:**
  - Solopreneur: If you have a unique skill set or expertise that allows you to handle most aspects of your business on your own then you can excel as a solopreneur.
  - Team Player: If you recognise your strengths but also acknowledge areas where others might be more skilled, you could be better suited for a team oriented role.
- **Risk Tolerance:**
  - Solopreneur: Solopreneurs often bear the full responsibility for their business success or failure. If you are comfortable with this risk then you are a solopreneur.
  - Team Player: In a team, the responsibilities are divided and this provides a sense of security. If you are ready to share both risks and rewards then you are a team player.
- **Communication and Collaboration:**
  - Solopreneur: If you find it difficult to communicate your vision or work with others, you prefer working on your own.
  - Team Player: If you enjoy brainstorming, networking and building relationships with others, then you are a team player.
- **Long-term Goals:**

- Solopreneur: If your long-term vision aligns with independent working and growing your business on your terms, then you are a solopreneur.
  - Team Player: If you are comfortable with working within an established organisation or contributing to larger group efforts, then you are a team player.
- **Flexibility and Adaptability:**
  - Solopreneur: You need adaptability as a solopreneur. If you have this trait and are ready for multitasking, then you are a solopreneur.
  - Team Player: In a team there is a well-defined role for each member. If you like stability and a well-defined role, then you are a team player.

However, with time your role can change and you may have to adapt as per the circumstances. Some may even make a transition from solopreneur to a team player.

Creating wealth as a solopreneur or a team player requires different approaches; however both paths can lead to financial success. Remember, it is self-awareness and adaptability that hold the key to choosing the role and by doing that you can focus your strength towards creating wealth.

Doctrine 54

Hidden Opportunities, Hidden Assets

IDENTIFYING HIDDEN OPPORTUNITIES in wealth creation can be a complex task, as it often involves discovering overlooked or unconventional strategies. Here are some avenues to explore potential hidden opportunities:

- **Value Investing:**
  Look for the undervalued assets in the stock market. Warren Buffett's approach is a classic example; one should earn by identifying stocks which are underrated or overlooked in a company's true worth.
- **Real Estate Distressed Properties:**
  Seek distressed properties that can be renovated and resold for a profit. Rehabilitation projects are always good opportunities.
- **Peer-to-Peer Lending:**
  Explore peer-to-peer lending platforms where you can lend money to individuals or small businesses in exchange for investment payments. This is a good source of alternative income.

- **Collectibles and Rare Items:**
  Invest in collectibles like art, vintage cars, rare stamps and coins, and even watches, where value can be appreciated over a period of time.
- **Cryptocurrency:**
  Research and invest in cryptocurrencies like Bitcoin and Ethereum. But, beware, as this is a very volatile category, and without research and a financial expert, one should not attempt this.
- **Eco-Friendly Investments:**
  Invest in companies that focus on sustainable and eco-friendly practices. This segment is growing and will be in high demand in the future.
- **Global Markets:**
  Explore international and emerging economy markets to look for investment opportunities.
- **Niche Startups:**
  Find out niche markets or innovative startups that solve unique problems or are trending in society.
- **Skills Development:**
  Invest in acquiring skills that are in high demand, such as coding, digital marketing, or data analysis, to increase your earning potential.

Remember that hidden opportunities always come with risks, so thorough research, due diligence, and risk management are necessary before attempting them. Also, don't forget to consult your financial advisor.

You have to be vigilant for finding these hidden assets. Always be alert and ready to grab the opportunities as they will be available briefly. There is a proverb for this, 'The opportunities God sends do not wake up those who are asleep.' If you are a treasure seeker, keep these things in mind:

- **Timing:**
  It is very crucial. As it is said, markets shift, fashion changes, and products fade.
- **Seriousness:**
  If you want it, you will get it. If you are not serious about these, the hidden assets will remain invisible to you.
- **Eccentricity:**
  You have to stand out to grab these. Be quirky, unique, special, and creative; think out of the box for this.
- **Clarity:**
  You should be clear about what you are doing. You should be well aware of all the positives and negatives. Do your SWOT analysis and in-depth research for each and every opportunity.

In conclusion, there are opportunities galore to help us make a fortune. All you have to do is to open up to those possibilities. Once you start noticing, you will get thousands of them.

Doctrine 55

Slow And Steady Wins The Race

WEALTH ACCUMULATION IS essentially a long-term endeavour. It requires consistent saving, smart investing, and financial discipline for many years to achieve significant wealth. Patience and a focus on long-term goals are the key aspects of this journey.

Throughout this book, I have insisted on a long-term perspective to create wealth. The longer you take to create wealth, the more diverse you can be with investments and income streams. The money that comes quickly goes out quicker as the foundation needed to build wealth is missing.

When you build wealth over time you are guarded against recession or sudden negative market downturns. You have a work-life balance. The wealth that you earn is honest and it gives you a long-term financial security.

When you make money too quickly it means you would spend it inappropriately as it would be difficult to handle. Moreover, quick money usually comes from a single source which denotes there is no diversity of risk.

Quick money often involves high risk and doesn't provide a solid foundation for building long-term wealth. Sustainable wealth is accumulated through careful financial planning, investing, and consistent saving over time.

If you want to walk on the path of wealth creation then you have to walk slowly and steadily because of the following:

- **Risk Diversity:**

    Quick money-making schemes are risky. Investment that promises quick returns often comes with the potential for significant losses. A slow and steady approach allows you to mitigate risk by diversifying your investments and making informed decisions over time.

- **Compound Interest:**

    Wealth can be built through the power of compound interest. Over time, your investment can earn interest on both the principal and the previously earned interest.

    The longer you invest, the more the power of compounding increases, resulting in exponential growth of your income.

- **Financial Discipline:**

    A slow and steady approach encourages financial discipline. The habit helps you to manage your finances responsibly and avoid impulsive or speculative decisions.

- **Knowledge Accumulation:**

    Building wealth requires knowledge and experience and it can be gained over time. Taking the time to learn about different investment opportunities, financial markets, and economic trends can lead to better decision-making. Also, knowledge compounds to wisdom over the years.

- **Reduced Emotional Stress:**

    Quick money also brings in high stress and anxiety. A

slow and steady approach helps reduce emotional stress because you are less likely to make rash decisions based on fear and greed.
- **Long-term Goals:**
Clear financial goals with a long-term perspective can help to gain wealth. This approach allows you to prioritise what truly matters to you, whether it is retirement, buying a new home, education, or other financial objectives.
- **Sustainable Wealth:**
Sustainable wealth can be built only on a strong foundation. It involves building a diversified portfolio of assets like stocks, bonds, real estate, and more. These assets can provide steady and regular income with growth potential, ensuring your wealth lasts for generations. It is not the speed but the direction that is more important. Similarly, consistency and repetition of the rate of growth is more important than the rate of growth.

Going slow and steady to create wealth is a prudent and sustainable approach. It minimises risks, harnesses the power of time and compound interest, and fosters financial discipline which allows you to make informed decisions.

It must be noted that true wealth is not a sprint; it is a marathon. Embrace the slow and steady journey, for it is the path to lasting prosperity. Though it takes time to see significant results, this approach is more likely to lead to lasting and meaningful wealth.

Doctrine 56
Beware Of Intruders

WHEN YOU HAVE money, you have to be watchful, as many would like to make inroads into your wealth.

How to safeguard your wealth from the big sharks circling around you? Watch out for the following:
- People offering money-making propositions.
- People offering to look after your money.
- People who are interested in your future or schemes.
- People offering financial advice.
- People offering work for you to double your money.
- People offering partnership.
- People offering products or services.

Be suspicious. Have a good due diligence strategy. There are many who will offer to make you rich quickly; beware of shortcuts and unethical practices. Be very cautious about offshore schemes, MLM schemes, and false and illegal schemes.

There are many who will offer to double your money. Beware of seed investments too. People who offer money for promotional materials or surveys are mostly after your money.

Make it a habit to ask the people who are offering anything to you, 'What is there for them?' and you might get your answer. Don't trust anyone blindly. Make informed financial decisions. Protect your wealth from all potential risks and scams. Your financial advisor/coach can warn you against common financial scams to safeguard your assets.

Protecting your wealth is like safeguarding a treasure; it requires vigilance, diversification, and wise counsel.

You have to keep in mind the following types of securities to protect your wealth:

- **Physical Security:**

    Home security systems, safes, and locks, CCTV systems—are some of the important tools you can use to protect your wealth.

- **Cybersecurity:**

    You have to protect your financial and personal information from online fraud. Strong unique passwords, two-factor authentications, and updated antivirus and other software are important. Don't click on unknown links and beware of phishing scams and unknown emails.

- **Banking Security:**

    Secure banking systems are utmost important. Use secure and reputed banks/financial institutions.

- **Identity Theft Protection:**

    Monitor your credit reports regularly for signs of identity theft. You can use identity theft protection services.

- **Encryption:**
  Encrypt all sensitive digital data and files to prevent unauthorised access. Use a password manager to secure your information.
- **Legal Protection:**
  Create safeguards like trusts and limited liability to protect your assets from potential lawsuits or creditors.
- **Privacy:**
  Be careful with social media and all your public appearances and dealings. Don't share any financial or personal information with strangers.
- **Insurance:**
  You should be fully insured against all kinds of theft, fraud, and other unexpected events. Identity Theft Insurance, homeowners, or rental insurance are important.
- **Shredding Documents:**
  Always shred financial documents, bills, statements before disposing off them to prevent identity theft.
- **Stay Informed:**
  Be informed about the latest security threats. Knowledge will help you prevent scams.
- **Legal Advisor:**
  Legal advice/knowledge is necessary to shield your wealth from potential intrusions.
- **Family Education:**
  Educate family members about security measures and other aspects of wealth protection.
- **Trustworthy Financial Advisor:**
  Work with trusted and reputed advisors only, and be careful about sharing financial information.

- **Emergency Plan:**
You should have an emergency plan for various scenarios, such as home invasion or cyber-attack, to ensure you and your family are protected.
- **Regular Review:**
All your security measures should be updated and reviewed regularly.

Remember, protecting wealth is more challenging than creating wealth. So make sure that you are taking good care of your hard-earned money and keeping it safely invested.

Doctrine 57

Your Money Should Work For You

MANY OF US waste our money by not making it work for us. Often, our money sits idly in savings accounts or low-yielding options and poor investments. We tend to value money that we haven't earned yet instead of the money we already have. Focusing on earning more can make us careless about what we already have. Most of us spend little/no time managing our earned money; instead, we always look for ways to earn more.

We all work very hard for money, but is our money working hard for us? In order to make money work for us, we need to train our minds and modify our money beliefs to always strive for real returns, and not just nominal returns. Let me explain real return again. In the context of investing, real return refers to the profit earned on an investment after adjusting inflation and taxes. This measure provides a more accurate picture of the investment's actual purchasing power over time. Unlike nominal returns, which only reflect the raw percentage gain or loss, real returns account for the eroding effects of inflation and the impact of taxes, offering a clearer view of the investment's true value. Understanding real return helps investors make more informed decisions by highlighting the actual growth of their wealth, rather than just the superficial gains.

Now, when you analyse the returns earned from savings accounts, fixed deposits, guaranteed plans (like traditional endowment plans from insurance companies), or poor investments, you'll find that they often yield zero or even negative real returns. This, in turn, erodes the purchasing power of your savings.

When you divide any country's population into categories—Employed, Self-Employed, Business Owners, and Investors—the majority will fall into the first two categories, that is, Employed and Self-Employed, comprising around 80 per cent or more. However, when you analyse the distribution of the country's income and wealth, it is exactly the opposite. The Employed and Self-Employed categories will hold only about 20 per cent, or even less, of the total wealth.

This table highlights the disparity between the population distribution and the wealth distribution among different employment categories.

Category	Percentage of Population	Percentage of Wealth
Employed	80% or more	20% or less
Self-Employed		
Business Owners	20% or less	80% or more
Investors		

What could be the reason for the disparities in wealth distribution among these four categories?

The key difference lies in how each group generates income. Employed and self-employed individuals work for money, while business owners and investors make money work for them.

Business owners and investors earn a significant portion of their income passively; their money generates more money without requiring constant effort. In contrast, employed and self-employed individuals rely almost entirely on active income, which involves trading their time for money. As long as you trade time for money, your earnings will be limited.

Moreover, if the savings from earned income do not generate positive real returns, it creates a vicious cycle of income and expense mismatch. This cycle can trap individuals in a never-ending loop where their purchasing power diminishes over time, making it harder to build wealth.

The journey to wealth creation begins with achieving positive real returns—the excess gains over taxes and inflation. Imagine your money as a diligent worker, tirelessly earning more for you. This is the magic of money earning money, which in turn boosts your purchasing power.

Consider this: if you invest Rs 1,000 and earn a nominal return of 10-12 per cent (post tax), but inflation is 6-7 per cent, your real return comes to around 4-6 per cent. That might seem modest, but it's the spark that ignites the fire of wealth creation. Over time, this excess gain compounds, and soon your money starts growing exponentially.

The key isn't chasing after massive returns but consistently achieving positive real returns. Think of it like planting a tree. You don't need a giant tree overnight; you need a sapling that grows steadily. Each rupee you invest should be like a seed, never left idle or unused, always deployed to fetch more.

But if you aim for very high returns and end up losing money, your wealth-building journey comes to a halt.

I'll conclude by saying, make your money work for you, so you don't have to work for your money. Consistency is crucial, but avoiding losses is even more essential. Remember, the power of compounding works best with steady, positive real returns. It's not about hitting home runs but about making sure every rupee is working hard for you, day in and day out.

Doctrine 58

Master The Art Of Exiting From An Investment

EVERYBODY HAS A different criteria for investment which largely depends on the financial goals. So we should have our norm on when to exit from an investment.

Before chalking out an exit plan, you should know some points which might help you:
- If the market is not right, have your exit plan ready.
- If you doubt your investment based on market information or feedback from your financial consultant, it's time to exit.
- You need money for better investment options. Once you have it, you can exit from your existing investment.

If the investment did not yield good returns despite waiting for long, then you should think of better options. You have achieved a handsome return on your investment, hence it is time to exit. But, the same is to be seen in a larger context, like any near-term financial requirement or alternate

investment option. Profit booking should never be solely on gain (return) alone.
- Switch to new avenues of investments if your traditional investment plan is not aligning with your investment goals.
- Relocate your funds if you want to diversify the risk as per the market conditions.
- If you don't have any information on your existing investments and it is getting difficult to predict the future, then it's time to exit.

There can be a number of reasons when you should not hold on to your investment. You should not continue your investment based on emotions. If returns are not good and the future looks bad, then there is no point in holding.

Market information and future trends are very important for any investment, so you must get all the information and seek advice from your financial advisor regularly. Build your investment portfolio slowly based on your experience, market knowledge, expert advice, and your own research. If the investment still does not look promising, then simply take an exit.

Sometimes we get information at the right time, but we don't exit from the investment due to emotions or simply laziness. So, whenever you get the information, act quickly.

Besides the investment performance, the exit timing will also depend on your financial goals and risk tolerance. Sometimes, you have to act according to the changing financial situation. Sometimes, due to tax considerations also, you have to exit from your current investment plan.

Mastering an exit plan requires careful consideration and a well thought out strategy. You can establish your unique exit criteria which you can follow strictly. An exit plan can be effective if your review system is efficient.

Keep a close eye on your investment. Regular review of performances, industry trends, and any relevant news/information which can impact your investment is utmost necessary.

For an exit plan, it is crucial to practice the 'what if' strategy discussed earlier. Consider various scenarios, such as unexpected developments. You can set up stop-loss orders in case of direct equity investment. You can also design a predetermined exit strategy based on set parameters.

Once your predefined exit criteria are met, execute your exit strategy promptly. Emotional decision-making can lead to a poor outcome in investing.

Remember, exiting an investment is not a sign of failure; it's a strategic decision that ensures your financial goals remain on course.

Doctrine 59

Know What Type Of Investor You Are

WE ALL HAVE tendencies to act on tips and market grapevines. We also act based on our emotions and greed, as far as investments are concerned. We are unable to exit when it is time, and we fail to enter when the time is right.

There are many different types of investors. In one of my investment videos, I have described the three types of investors based on the years of investment they put in:

- **Beginner**
  This type of investor has just begun the investment journey with a beginner's mindset and temperament. They need different types of investment advice and investment tools.[6]

- **Mature**
  These types of investors have been in their investment journey for over 5 to 10 years, so they have a good insight

---

[6] Video: Beginners Guide to Investing, Video Link: https://youtu.be/dEU6QB_eDlM?si=s1hv9qWOkff7K0hV

into investment rules, and they understand the nitty-gritty of investments. These types of investors need a unique set of an investment plan and strategy.[7]

- **Pro**
This type of investors have a good corpus of investment, and they have tried and tested all kinds of investment plans and strategies. They have a good insight, and they have mastered the trade. As they know almost everything, they now need to unlearn and re-learn to scale new heights.[8]

I designed the above categories for suggesting them various investment plans. As per their category, each one of them has unique financial goals and risk appetite.

'Money is an emotional instrument, but emotions can get in the way of making the right investment decisions. If we can fathom our individual emotional tendencies, then we can take steps to anticipate and correct them.'—Hannah Grove (Chief Marketing Officer, Merrill Lynch Investment)

Investing is not just about numbers and charts; it's also deeply influenced by our personalities and psychological traits. Merrill Lynch has identified several types of investor based on these aspects. Let's dive into these profiles and see which one resonates with you:

- **Confident Investors**: These investors are self-assured and they often make decisions based on their own research and analysis. They tend to be more risk-tolerant and are comfortable with market volatility.

---

[7] Video: Who is a Mature Investor I Rules That a Mature Investor Should follow, Video Link: https://youtu.be/B_KVSJTTwBA?si=b6kUbq8BIQi9JMPD

[8] Video: Who is a Pro Investor [Rules That a Pro Investor Should follow, Video Link: https://youtu.be/Af-6_vDbqyw?si=fpId26vyRFoDNH9J

- **Anxious Investors**: These individuals are more risk-averse and they often worry about market fluctuations. They may frequently check their investments and are more likely to seek advice from financial experts to feel secure.
- **Impulsive Investors**: Characterised by their quick decision-making, these investors may act on market trends or tips without thorough research. They are prone to buying high and selling low due to emotional reactions.
- **Cautious Investors**: These investors prefer to take a conservative approach, focusing on preserving capital rather than seeking high returns. They often invest in low-risk assets and are meticulous in their research.
- **Analytical Investors**: These individuals rely heavily on data and detailed analysis before making investment decisions. They are methodical and hence they prefer a systematic approach to investing.

Understanding these psychological profiles can help investors recognise their own biases and make more informed decisions.

Investors are also classified by their investing style. Investing is like choosing a path in a vast financial landscape. Each path represents a different investment style, and finding the one that suits you best can make your journey more rewarding. Let's explore some popular investment styles in a simple and engaging way.

Value Investing

- **What is it**: This style focuses on finding undervalued stocks that are trading below their intrinsic value. Think

of it as hunting for hidden gems in the stock market.
- **Who is it For**: If you have patience and a keen eye for detail, value investing might be your style. It's about buying quality companies at a bargain and holding them until their true value is recognised. This approach can also be applied to other financial assets and even spending habits. It encourages thoughtful decision-making and long-term value creation across various aspects of one's financial life.

Growth Investing
- **What is it**: Growth investors seek companies with strong potential for future growth. These are often companies in emerging industries or those with innovative products.
- **Who is it For**: If you're excited about the future and willing to take on more risk for the possibility of higher returns, growth investing could be your path. It's about riding the wave of innovation and expansion.

Income Investing
- **What is it:** This style focuses on generating a steady income through dividends or interest payments or rental income. It's like planting a money tree that provides regular fruit.
- **Who is it For:** If you prefer stability and regular income, income investing is ideal for you. It's popular among retirees or those looking for a reliable cash flow.

Index Investing
- **What is it**: Index investors buy a broad market index, like the S&P 500, to mirror the market's performance. It's a

passive investment strategy.
- **Who is it for**: If you believe in the long-term growth of the market and prefer a hands-off approach, index investing is a great choice. It's simple, cost-effective, and diversified.

Active Trading
- **What is it**: Active traders buy and sell stocks frequently to capitalise on short-term market movements. It's a dynamic and fast-paced style.
- **Who is it for**: If you enjoy the thrill of the market and have the time to monitor it closely, active trading might be for you. It's about making quick decisions and staying on top of trends.

Socially Responsible Investing
- **What is it**: It focuses on investing in companies that align with ethical, social, and environmental values. It's about making a positive impact with your money.
- **Who is it for**: If you want your investments to reflect your values and contribute to a better world, this style is the way to go. It's about balancing profit with purpose.

Choosing an investment profile is like finding a pair of shoes that fit perfectly. It should align with your financial goals, risk tolerance, and personal preferences. You may even find a combination of profiles working best for you.

Remember, investing is a journey, and your profile may evolve over time as you gain experience and your financial situation changes. The key is to start with a profile or a combination that feels right for you; be open to learning and adapting along the way.

There are times when transitioning from one investor profile to another may not be feasible. Investing and wealth creation are not solo endeavours; they require a collaborative effort. Building a strong network, forming diverse circles, and hiring competent consultants and experts can provide crucial support in various circumstances.

Understanding your core strengths is vital, but equally important is recognising your limitations and weaknesses. You can address these through continuous learning or by outsourcing tasks to professionals, or a combination of both. One of the biggest challenges for anyone is to admit 'I don't know'. Often, we fall into the trap of pretending to know everything, which prevents us from acknowledging our gaps in knowledge. This can lead to misguided actions, missed opportunities, and financial losses.

Embracing humility and seeking help when needed can significantly enhance your investment journey and lead to better financial outcomes. It is crucial to understand yourself as an investor, for it is not a one-time process but a continuous journey requiring ongoing introspection.

Doctrine 60

Dancing With The Financial Statements

TO ACHIEVE WEALTH, abundance, and contentment, it's essential to know where we stand financially. Understanding our strengths and weaknesses, identifying key areas for improvement, and taking corrective actions are crucial. Direction matters more than speed in our financial journey. Regularly assessing our financial health, ideally every six months and quarterly as wealth grows, ensures we stay on the right path. This chapter will guide you through the key financial statements and metrics to help you navigate your financial journey effectively.

A personal financial statement provides a snapshot of an individual's financial position at a specific point in time and tracks their financial journey over time. It includes details on income and expenses, assets and liabilities, and net worth. These statements are essential for tracking financial goals, managing wealth, and handling debt effectively.

Types of Financial Statements:
Personal Income and Expense Statement
- A financial document that shows your earnings and expenditures over a specific period.
- **Components:**
  - **Income**: Includes salary, fees, business profits, interest, gains, dividends, etc.
  - **Expenses**: Covers utilities, groceries, rent, interest, etc.
- **Purpose**:
  - Tracks cash flow and aids in budgeting.
  - Provides a clear picture of income sources and spending patterns.
  - Facilitates better and more effective financial decisions.
  - Is essential for planning and tracking financial goals.

Personal Balance Sheet
- A financial document that lists all assets (what you own) and liabilities (what you owe).
- **Components**:
  - **Assets**: Land, buildings, cash, advances, equity, jewellery, vehicles, investments, etc.
  - **Liabilities**: Home loan, business loan, personal loan, credit card outstanding, etc.
- **Purpose**:
  - Shows the balance between assets and liabilities, helping to calculate your net worth.
  - Allows you to track financial progress over time by observing changes in net worth.
  - Serves as a foundation for budgeting, investing, and planning future goals, resulting into more effective

and informed financial decisions.
- o Important for assessing your monetary value and credit worthiness.

Investment Report
- A financial report that provides detailed information about your investment portfolio, including holdings, performance, and gains or losses over time.
- **Components**:
  - o **Investment Portfolio**: Includes all savings and investments such as fixed deposits, insurance policies, shares, bonds, debentures, provident funds, commodities, etc.
- **Purpose**:
  - o Evaluates the performance of each investment against objectives and benchmarks.
  - o Consolidated Performance offers a comprehensive view of the entire portfolio's performance, highlighting top and bottom contributors and assessing the real return of the portfolio as a whole and its individual components.
  - o Provides strategic insights into the effectiveness of investment strategies and decision-making processes.
  - o Identifies potential risks and opportunities for improvement.
  - o Tracks the growth and changes in the investment portfolio over time.

Analysing a Personal Financial Statement
Once you have drafted your financial statements, the next critical step is to analyse them effectively to grasp the core

essence of your financial well-being. To do this optimally, categorise the components of each statement and analyse their composition and changes over time.

Income and Expense Statement
- **Income:** Divide income into Earned Income (income from work) and Passive Income (interest, dividends, gains, royalties). As you progress in life, aim to increase the proportion of passive income to achieve financial freedom. The goal should be to grow passive income rather than just earning more.
- **Expenses:**
  o **Fixed Expenses:** Recurring costs that remain constant, such as rent, insurance premiums, salaries, wages, memberships, and subscriptions.
  o **Variable Expenses:** Costs that fluctuate based on usage, like utility bills and fuel.
  o **Discretionary Expenses:** Non-essential costs that can be adjusted or eliminated, such as entertainment, travel, and dining out.
- **Net Income:** The surplus or deficit between income and expenses. Surplus funds should be allocated to savings or investments, while deficits may need to be covered by loans.

Balance Sheet
- **Assets:**
  o **Fixed Assets:** Tangible items that provide ownership experience and can be displayed, such as land, buildings, vehicles, jewellery, and commodities.
  o **Financial Assets:** Intangible items like fixed

deposits, bank balances, bonds, shares, and digital assets. Fixed assets are often illiquid and have higher maintenance costs.
- **Liabilities:**
  - **Short-term Debts:** Obligations that need to be repaid within days, months, or a year, such as advances, friendly loans, overdrafts, and dues.
  - **Long-term Debts:** Debts repaid over years, typically through EMIs (Equated Monthly Installments). Short-term liabilities require larger liquidity for repayment, while long-term debts incur high interest costs over time.
- **Net Worth:** The difference between assets and liabilities, representing the monetary value of an individual. Focus on increasing net worth by adding assets and reducing liabilities to enhance passive income and achieve financial freedom.

Investment Report

- **Understand Holdings Composition:** Begin by categorising your investments into asset classes such as equity, debt, real estate, and commodities, and by duration (short, medium, and long-term). This helps assess the diversification and risk profile of your portfolio.
- **Evaluate Performance:** Measure the overall profitability of your holdings in percentage terms rather than simple multipliers. This allows for fair performance comparisons across different investments and asset classes. Include both capital gains (increase in asset value) and income (dividends or interest) in your evaluation.
- **Assess Gains and Losses**: Distinguish between realised

and unrealised gains/losses. Realised gains/losses come from sold holdings and affect your taxable income, providing a clear picture of actual financial outcomes. Unrealised gains/losses are potential profits/losses on holdings still held, reflecting current market value and fluctuating over time. Tracking both is crucial for tax planning and informed decision-making about buying or selling assets.

- **Monitor Consistently**: Regularly review your investment report to stay updated on performance and market conditions, but avoid overly frequent checks. Ensure your portfolio is well-diversified to manage risk and optimise returns.
- **Rebalance Periodically**: Adjust your portfolio periodically to maintain your desired asset allocation and risk level.
- **Focus on Financial Goals:** Avoid evaluating your investment report solely based on returns. Chasing the highest returns or competing with peers can lead to higher risk, poor outcomes, disappointment, and stress. Instead, align your evaluation with your financial goals and personal risk profile.

By following these steps, you can gain a comprehensive understanding of your investments, make informed decisions, and work towards achieving your financial goals.

Importance of Each Financial Statement
- **Income and Expense Statement**
  - Budgeting and financial planning
  - Identifying spending patterns

- Managing cash flow
- **Balance Sheet**
  - Evaluating financial stability
  - Planning for future financial goals
  - Understanding asset allocation
  - Measuring financial progress
  - Setting and achieving financial goals
  - Understanding overall financial health
- **Investment Report**
  - Tracking investment performance
  - Making informed investment decisions
  - Assessing risk and return

Understanding How Gains are Measured

Measuring gains in percentage rather than multiples is crucial for clarity, comparison, and analysis. Understanding different types of returns and their applicability enables sound financial decisions and avoids misunderstandings.

Absolute Return

Also known as total return, it is the difference between the current value and purchase value in percentage. It does not account for the time taken to achieve the return, making it simple to calculate and useful for measuring short-term gains (less than a year). For example, if you buy a stock for Rs 10,000 and its value increases to Rs 15,000, the absolute return is 50 per cent.

Annual Return

This is the percentage gain or loss of an investment over a one-year period. It provides a standardised way to assess how well an investment has performed over a year, making it easier to compare different investments. However, it does not consider compounding, which can lead to an overestimation of actual returns. For example, if you invest Rs 1,00,000 and it grows to Rs 1,20,000 in one year, then the annual return is 20 per cent.

Compounded Annual Growth Rate (CAGR)
CAGR represents the mean annual growth rate of an investment over a specified period longer than one year. It smooths out volatility and fluctuations, making it easier to understand an investment's true annual growth rate. By standardising growth rates, CAGR allows for a fair comparison between different assets, regardless of their varying growth rates over time. It aids in setting realistic financial goals and planning by helping investors estimate the future value of their investments. For example, if an investment grows from Rs 1,00,000 to Rs 1,50,000 over 3 years, the CAGR is 14.47 per cent.

Extended Internal Rate of Return (XIRR)
XIRR is a method to calculate the annualised return of an investment with irregular cash flows. It uses a series of cash flows (both positive and negative) and their corresponding dates to compute the return. XIRR provides a precise calculation of the annualised rate of return for investments with irregular cash flows, accounting for the timing and amount of each cash flow. For SIPs, recurring deposits, life insurance premiums, and other financial instruments with irregular cash flows, XIRR offers a clear understanding of the impact of such flows on the overall return and is useful for

evaluating true performance over time. For instance, if you invest Rs 1,00,000 on 1 January 2021, and then Rs 50,000 on 1 July 2022, and receive Rs 1,80,000 on 31 December 2023, XIRR will calculate the annualised return considering these irregular cash flows, which is approximately 16.08 per cent.

Understanding these different types of returns helps investors evaluate the performance of their investments more accurately. Absolute return provides a straightforward measure of profit or loss; annual return standardises performance over a year; CAGR smooths out growth rates over multiple years, and XIRR handles investments with irregular cash flows. By using these metrics, investors can make more informed decisions and better achieve their financial goals.

Important Ratios to Monitor
- **Liquidity Ratios**
  - Current Ratio, Quick Ratio
  - Importance: Assessing short-term financial health
- **Leverage Ratios**
  - Debt-to-Equity Ratio, Debt Ratio
  - Importance: Understanding financial risk
- **Profitability Ratios**
  - Return on Equity (ROE), Net Profit Margin
  - Importance: Evaluating profitability
- **Efficiency Ratios**
  - Asset Turnover Ratio, Inventory Turnover
  - Importance: Assessing operational efficiency
- **Market Value Ratios**
  - Price-to-Earnings (P/E) Ratio, Earnings Per Share (EPS)
  - Importance: Valuing investments

Evaluating Personal Financial Health Through Key Ratios

Understanding your personal financial health is crucial, much like monitoring your physical health through regular checkups. Financial statements provide a wealth of information, but to truly grasp your financial status, you need to evaluate specific ratios. These ratios act like key indicators in a medical report, highlighting important signals and focus areas for action. The primary ratios to consider are the liquidity ratio, net worth ratio, and debt-to-income ratio.

Liquidity Ratio

The liquidity ratio indicates your ability to meet sudden large cash outflow due to any contingency or unforeseen circumstance without having to incur cost of borrowing or disposing productive assets. To determine the liquidity ratio, you need to calculate how many months of expenses can be covered by your cash assets in the event of a loss of income.

Liquidity Ratio = Cash Assets/Monthly Expenses

Cash assets shall include bank balance, bank fixed deposits, cash on hand and debt mutual funds.

If you have Rs 1,50,000 in cash assets and your monthly expenses are Rs 30,000, your liquidity ratio will be Rs 1,50,000/30,000 = 5, that is in absence of any income your cash assets can cover 5 months of expenses. Ideally, the ratio should be 6-2 times of monthly expenses, which will keep you prepared for any unforeseen expenses and contingencies.

Savings Ratio

This ratio indicates how much portion of income is retained post meeting all expenses. It is calculated by dividing total savings by gross income. If your annual saving mount is Rs 2,00,000 and your gross income is Rs 10,00,000, your savings ratio will be Rs 2,00,000/10,00,000 = 0.20 or 20 per cent. It means you are saving 20 per cent of your gross income for future needs and goals. Gross income shall include all type of earnings, like salary, business or professional income, bonus, interest, rent, dividend, gains and royalty. Ideal ratio depends on the work profile and life stage.

Life Stage	Ideal Savings Ratio
Single	50%
Married	30%
After Children	20%

Debt-to-Income Ratio

This ratio measures the portion of your monthly income used for debt repayments. It's calculated by dividing your monthly debt payments (EMI) by your monthly gross income. This ratio helps assess your ability to manage debt without undue stress or risk of default. For example, if your monthly debt payments are Rs 20,000 and your gross income is Rs 80,000, your DTI ratio is 25 per cent (Rs 20,000/80,000). Ideally, this ratio should not exceed 30 per cent, as higher values can lead to difficulties in managing debt, especially with rising interest rates or falling income.

Debt to Asset Ratio

It measures your financial health by comparing your liabilities to your assets. It helps determine if you are over-borrowing and funding your lifestyle through loans, which can lead to repayment challenges. This ratio is calculated by dividing total liabilities by total assets. Liabilities include all borrowings, like home loans, car loans, personal loans, and any dues to friends and family. Assets include cash, property, jewellery, deposits, and equities. For a more accurate financial assessment, consider excluding property and jewellery from your assets. An ideal debt-to-asset ratio is 50 per cent, meaning your liabilities should be half of your assets.

Personal Net Worth Ratio
The Personal Net Worth Ratio is a financial metric that indicates how much of your assets are financed by earned income versus debt.
- Net Worth: The difference between total assets and total liabilities.
- Calculation: Net Worth Ratio=Total Assets/Net Worth

For example, if you have assets worth Rs 1 crore and liabilities of Rs 60 lakhs, your net worth is Rs 40 lakhs. The personal net worth ratio would be Rs 1,00,00,000/40,00,000 =0.40 or 40 per cent.

This means 40 per cent of your total assets are financed by your income, while 60 per cent is financed by debt. A lower ratio suggests higher reliance on borrowed money, while a higher ratio indicates greater reliance on earned income.

Additionally, the net worth ratio can be measured by dividing net worth by annual income:

Net Worth Ratio=Annual Income/Net Worth

For instance, if your net worth is Rs 40 lakhs and your annual income is Rs 50 lakhs, the ratio would be:

Rs 50,00,000/40,00,000=0.80
Ideally, this ratio should be 1 per cent or higher.

Insurance Coverage Ratio
Death, disability and disease are the three risks applicable to all of us, but its time and impact can never be ascertained accurately. Though their occurrence is random and unknown, their financial impact on self and family is deep and can really have life changing effects. So what do you do for these risk, which are certain but we are not sure of their occurrence nor the extent of financial loss? Well, a wise answer is to have insurance cover for all these risks rather than being optimistic that 'I will not be the One'. Ideally, one should have life insurance and disability coverage around 10-20 times of annual income. In case of health insurance, one can get coverage equivalent to a year's income. There are many complex workings to ascertain one's ideal coverage but the above mentioned is a thumb rule. One should be adequately insured, neither under nor over. The cost of premium against the cover is quite a small price to pay against the bigger unknown risk.

Insurance Coverage Ratios: Safeguarding Your Financial Well-Being
1. **Life Insurance Coverage**:
    o **Purpose**: Provides financial security for your family in case of your untimely demise.
    o **Ideal Coverage**: Aim for 10-20 times your annual income.
    o **Caution**: Purchase life insurance as a standalone product from a reputable insurer rather than as a rider

on a life insurance policy.
2. **Disability Insurance Coverage**:
   - **Purpose**: Safeguards your income if you're unable to work due to injury.
   - **Ideal Coverage**: Approximately 10-20 times your annual income.
   - **Caution**: Consider disability insurance as a separate policy, not just a rider on another plan.
3. **Critical Illness Cover**:
   - **Purpose**: Protects against loss of income due to serious illnesses (such as cancer, heart disease).
   - **Ideal Coverage**: Aim for 1-2 years of your annual income.
   - **Why?**: Critical illnesses can disrupt your ability to work, affecting your financial stability.
4. **Health Insurance**:
   - **Purpose**: Covers medical expenses, ensuring quality healthcare without financial strain.
   - **Ideal Coverage**: Consider at least one year's income. For example, if you earn Rs 8 lakhs annually, opt for a Rs 8 lakhs health insurance policy.
   - **Why?**: Shields you from rising medical costs and provides peace of mind.

Remember, adequate insurance is a small price to pay for the security it offers against life's uncertainties. Don't be underinsured or overinsured; maintain a balance and protect your future wisely.

In conclusion, financial statements play a crucial role in understanding the strength, weakness and the growth potential of an individual's finances. One can gauge the current position of funds and make decisions accordingly. This makes financial statements an imperative in the revenue assessment and decision-making process.

Doctrine 61

It's All About Taxes

ONE SHOULD NEVER try to evade paying taxes. However, there is a difference between evading taxes and avoiding taxes. When you have enough money, it is important to avoid taxes. You should consult a good and professional tax consultant to plan your taxes better.

When you earn more money, your tax issues get increasingly complex. Since the taxation laws keep changing, one should stay updated to save taxes.

Saving taxes is crucial to financial planning and should be done within the legal limit. There are ways and strategies you can follow for a tax efficient wealth creation:

- **Invest With The Tax Planning:**
  Choose tax efficient investment schemes so that you generate lower taxable income. Long-term investments receive more favourable tax treatment.
- **Tax Loss Harvesting:**
  Offset gains with losses in your investment portfolio to

reduce your tax liabilities.

- **Long-term Investment:**
Capital gain taxes are usually lower for assets held over a year. Choose a long-term investment strategy to benefit from these lower rates.
- **Diversify Your Portfolio:**
A diversified portfolio can help spread risk and reduce tax liabilities. Different types of assets may have different tax treatments.
- **Use Tax Credits and Deductions:**
Use tax deduction and credits for which you qualify. It depends on your personal circumstances and can significantly reduce your tax burden.
- **Estate Planning:**
Plan your estate to minimise taxes for your heirs. Strategies, like gifting, trust and use of the estate, and tax exemption among others, can be valuable.
- **Consult a Tax Expert:**
Tax laws are complex and dynamic. Consult a tax advisor or financial planner who can provide a personalised advice based on your specific situation.
- **Have a Limited Company:**
Limited Company can attract less tax and can give all sorts of options which are not available for the self-employed. Remember that while tax saving is important, it should be in sync with your wealth building strategy and long-term financial goals, risk tolerance and investor horizon. Also, though income comes before tax, our money beliefs wire us to think first about tax.

Rememebr, every rupee you save in taxes is another rupee you can invest in building your wealth. Every penny counts. Consider tax saved as money earned. So, pay due attention to your taxes and make sure you have a competent tax consultant to help you navigate.

Doctrine 62

Assets—Make Them Work For You!

IN THIS DOCTRINE we will explore the concept of assets and their role in building wealth. Assets are the foundation of financial freedom, and understanding how to leverage them effectively is crucial. Whether you're just starting your financial journey or looking to optimise your existing assets, these principles will guide you toward financial success.

Assets vs Liabilities
Rethinking the Belief
Traditionally, we've been conditioned to think of assets as what we own and liabilities as what we owe. However, a more nuanced perspective is essential for financial success. Consider this revised understanding:

- **Assets:** Assets are not just possessions; they are income generators. They bring money into your life. Examples include investments, like shares, mutual funds, real estate, and business ownership.
- **Liabilities:** Liabilities, on the other hand, take money

away from you. They create expenses. Debts, loans, and high-maintenance possessions fall into this category.

Let's break down common personal assets:
1. **Financial Assets:**
   o **Cash:** Currency in hand.
   o **Deposits:** Savings accounts, fixed deposits, company deposit, etc.
   o **Investments:** Stocks, mutual funds, bonds, and REITs.
   o **Insurance Policies:** Life insurance, health insurance, etc.
2. **Physical Assets:**
   o **Real Estate:** Homes, land, commercial properties.
   o **Vehicles:** Cars, motorcycles, etc.
   o **Jewellery:** Precious metals and gemstones.
3. **Other Assets:**
   o **Advances:** Money lent to others.
   o **Intellectual Property:** Copyrights, patents, trademarks.

Productive vs Non-Productive Assets
Productive Assets
Productive assets create income and grow your wealth. Their key characteristics include:
- **Income Generation:** They earn interest, dividends, or capital gains.
- **Low Maintenance:** They don't require significant ongoing expenses. Examples include dividend-paying stocks, rental properties, and well-managed businesses.

Non-Productive Assets

Non-productive assets lack income potential and may even drain resources. They are characterised by:

- **No Income Generation:** They don't contribute to your financial growth.
- **Maintenance Costs:** Frequent expenses for upkeep. For example, residence, farm house, luxury items (like high-end jewellery, accessories, watch), collectibles, and some personal vehicles.

Let's delve into some important aspects of ownership, focusing on house, car, and jewellery:

- **House**

  A house is a significant part of an individual's financial statement, providing ownership, security, and social status. While it represents financial success, it doesn't generate income. You might argue it saves rent and offers peace of mind, but expenses, like interest, maintenance, taxes, and repairs, often exceed the notional rent saved. Buying real estate is easy, but selling it can be challenging. Would you sell your house to book gains and move to a smaller one? Many get stuck in the financial rat race by buying a house too soon or beyond their budget. It's crucial to own a house, but not in a haste or at any cost—especially not by sacrificing liquidity and most of your earnings and assets. Ideally, your house should be three times your annual income. If your current income isn't that high, consider your debt-to-income ratio and future income growth to match the purchase, as it will be funded by taking loan.

- **Car**
  A car is both a utility and a symbol of pride, a dream for many. While you can't display your income tax return or salary slip, your car serves as a means of travel and a display of financial success and wealth. However, it also significantly drains your income due to fuel, repairs, maintenance, driver costs, interest, and depreciation. When selling or replacing it, you often get much less than the purchase price. We tend to replace cars with bigger and more expensive models, leading to even greater depreciation losses in the future. Most people decide on the size and type of car based on their future income, thinking a slightly higher EMI will get them a bigger car. This practice results in a huge opportunity cost due to missed savings and investments, increasing monthly expenses and cash outflow. It also leads to overspending and increased financial stress and insecurity. Ideally, one should buy a car based on their net worth, especially financial assets, rather than monthly income.
- **Jewellery**
  While the value of precious metals and stones can appreciate over time, jewellery comes with significant making costs, which are a substantial part of the purchase price and are lost when you sell. Additionally, jewellery incurs storage costs, such as bank locker fees, and maintenance costs, like polishing and repairs. Moreover, people rarely sell jewellery to book gains. It is more often seen as a form of consumption, passed down through generations, and seldom sold for liquidity, except in critical circumstances.

While items like houses, cars, and jewellery constitute a significant portion of an individual's personal balance sheet, they don't inherently increase your income. In fact, they often add to your expenses, leading to a perpetual cycle of working harder for money.

Similarly, cash, bank balances, and idle deposits lose purchasing power over time due to inflation. They rarely generate post-tax returns greater than inflation, making these assets unproductive and failing to contribute significantly to your wealth.

Investing in productive assets that outpace inflation and compound over time is crucial for building wealth. Good real estate, quality business shares, and equity mutual funds fall into this category. These productive assets yield returns higher than inflation, boosting both your income and purchasing power.

When you draw your balance sheet with this classification, you'll gain a true and clear picture of your financial standing. You may realise that many assets you have acquired are actually liabilities disguised as assets, as they do not add to your income, but increase your expenses.

The Pursuit of Wealth: A Life-Altering Choice
When we embark on our earning journey, we encounter three distinct paths—Safety, Comfort, and Wealth. Most people instinctively choose safety—a secure job or profession. Once that safety net is in place, comfort beckons. Houses, cars, and material possessions become markers of status. As income grows, so does the pursuit of comfort, leaving little room for wealth-building.

But here's the twist: by the time we realise what truly

matters for a meaningful life, our earning years are limited. Many fall into the trap of seeking quick wealth, enticed by promises of big returns, only to find themselves stressed and disillusioned, making losses instead of gains. Others swing to the opposite extreme, embracing austerity, limiting their lifestyle, and compromising their golden years.

Old age poverty often stems from financial illiteracy, the inability to distinguish assets from liabilities. But, there's hope. Those who choose the third path, wealth, right from the beginning, are more likely to attain financial freedom. They don't sacrifice comfort, instead, they prioritise productive assets. Later, comfort flows naturally, funded by their wealth.

In conclusion, own assets that work for you, and not the other way around. Assets, when wisely chosen and prudently managed, have the remarkable ability to labour silently and persistently to create wealth on your behalf.

Doctrine 63

Know Your Worth

IF YOU ARE a professional, businessman or in service, you should know your worth. Knowing your worth is important as you get your money based on your worth. Knowing your worth means knowing your price. Unless and until you are confident of your price, you cannot trade it against your services.

Knowing your worth can have a significant impact on your ability to create wealth in many ways such as:

- **Negotiation Power:**
  Understanding your skills, expertise and the value you can create will enable you to negotiate better for your fees, salaries and contracts. This can lead to higher earnings and more opportunities for wealth accumulation.
- **Investment Power:**
  When you trust your abilities you are more likely to invest in your core competence, education, training and entrepreneurship. These investments help you to

create wealth.

- **Entrepreneurship:**
  When you have confidence in your worth it helps you to start your own business. Believing in your product or services value can attract customers and investors thereby helping you grow and generate wealth.
- **Risk Appetite:**
  Knowing your worth can make you more willing to take calculated risks in your career or investments which can lead to generating more money.
- **Networking:**
  When you know your value, you become more confident and it helps you to connect with like-minded people, mentors, consultants and potential business partners or clients. This network can open the door for you to create wealth.
- **Financial Planning:**
  A strong sense of self-worth can help you to make better financial decisions. You are more likely to save, invest and manage your finances wisely when you believe you deserve financial security and success.
- **Self-Investment:**
  Knowing your worth motivates you to prioritise self-improvement through personal development, new skills learning, and exploring possibilities for higher earnings.

We can conclude by underlining the fact that recognising your worth can boost your confidence, empower you to make strategic decisions and create opportunities that lead to greater wealth accumulation. It is a mindset which helps you to create wealth. If you know your worth, wealth will follow. When you value your skills, time and contributions, you open the door to opportunities that lead to financial success.

Doctrine 64

Think Out Of The Box

WEALTH CREATION IS a creative pursuit. And like all creative journeys, you have to think out of the box and travel on the path which is less travelled.

When you observe the wealthy people and study their journey, you will notice that they have all achieved their wealth in a very unique way.

It requires a lot of courage, dedication, confidence and maturity to think differently and go on a different path. If you follow the crowd, you may end up in distress. You have to get out of your herd mentality. When the crowd is chasing something, you have to come out of that rat race.

Creating wealth and protecting it is a creative endeavour, involving innovative thinking, problem solving, and ability to seize opportunities others may overlook.

If you adopt a creative route to create wealth, it will be a wonderful journey and you will like all its ups and down. The creative process of wealth creation calls for:

- **Innovation**

  Many successful people have created wealth by innovating. The innovative way to create wealth involves creating new products, services or business models that either address unmet needs or solve problems in a unique way.

  Innovation can stem from existing ideas or entirely new concepts. There are many examples such as Uber, Airbnb, Zomato, and Apple among others. But you should look around and note down the innovations around you. Don't confuse innovation with invention. Innovation is applicable to existing things; it is simply about finding a more better or efficient way to do the same thing. You don't always need to do different things, you can just find a different way.

- **Problem Solving**

  Wealth creation often starts with identifying a problem or a gap in the market. Entrepreneurs use their creativity to find solutions that solve the problem or the unmet needs and generate values out of it.

- **Be Adaptable and Receptive**

  The business landscape is constantly changing. You have to adapt to this changing environment and undergo evolution to create wealth. You have to be receptive enough to understand the changing consumer preferences, trends and demand curves. This will ensure that your wealth flows in automatically.

- **It's All About Risk-Taking**

  Calculated risk-taking is the backbone of wealth creation. You have to take risks to explore new opportunities. Besides taking risks, you have to manage them, too.

Entrepreneurs and investors must creatively assess and mitigate risks to protect their wealth. This involves thinking out of the box to identify the potential pitfalls and develop contingency plans accordingly.
- **Creating Values**
Wealth creation is the outcome of value creation through products, services, or investments. This value creation process needs creativity to identify unique selling points, enhance customer experiences, and stand out in a competitive market.
- **Collaboration**
Collaboration is the new mantra of success in a competitive market. Joint ventures, strategic alliance, partnership and investment networks are some of the examples of collaboration. Creativity in building and maintaining these relationships holds the key to wealth creation.
- **Continuous Learnings**
Successful wealth creators are lifelong learners. They learn about everyone and everything. Likewise, you have to keep yourself updated with financial markets, industry trends and investment strategies. You have to develop a creative mindset to adapt and absorb new information.

Remember, just as an artist creates a masterpiece following a creative process, similarly an individual can craft financial success using creative strategies. Creativity is the brush, strategy the canvas, and action the strokes that paint the masterpiece of wealth.

Doctrine 65

You Are Rich As It Is Your Right To Be Rich

WHILE PENNING DOWN this book, I met a wealthy person who has devoted his post-retirement life to philanthropy. He is passionately working for the underprivileged in the field of health, education and creating self-awareness among the youth. My discussions with him gave me some profound insights on creating and protecting wealth. Listed below are some of my key takeaways from our discussion:

- You have a fundamental right to be rich. You are here in this universe to live a life of abundance, happiness, joy and freedom. You should, therefore, have all the money you need to lead a happy and prosperous life.
- Money is just a symbol of health. When your blood is freely circulating in your body, you are healthy. When money is freely circulating in your life, you are economically healthy.
- When people hoard money, they get charged with fear and greed and become economically ill.
- You are making a wrong choice if earning money is your

sole aim. Your focus should be on expressing your talent, pursuing your passion, and making your family happy while doing something worthwhile for the society at large. To do all this, you need resources like money, efforts and time.

'Money is only a tool. It will take you wherever you wish, but it will not replace you as the driver.'—Ayn Rand

So, don't waste all your time in earning money; spend time in following your passion and goal. Money will flow automatically.

- Poverty is a mental illness. Physical illness means something ails your body and you try to improve your condition. Similarly, if you are not earning enough, or have a shortage of money circulating in your life, it hampers your mental well-being. Similarly, your ill beliefs are restricting you from earning in abundance and keeping you poor. Any illness needs to be treated physically and emotionally, so get your beliefs aligned towards abundance and take prompt actions.
- You should never criticise money, as you lose what you condemn. You cannot attract what you criticise.
- Protect your investment. Do this simple self-suggestion exercise by repeating: 'Infinite intelligence governs and watches over all my financial transactions. Whatever I do, shall prosper.'
- You cannot get something for nothing. Build a character to build wealth. Don't steal, but try to create. With honesty, integrity and perseverance, you can build wealth.
- You must give to receive. Whatever you give, you receive in multiples.
- If you want to sell a property, practice affirming: 'The

infinite intelligence attracts to me the buyer for this property, who wants it, and who prospers in it.'
- Successful and rich people are not selfish; they want to serve the mankind.

In this book, I have repeated all these psychological points about money and wealth. Once you start implementing these doctrines you will be amazed to see the results.

Doctrine 66

Securing Your Legacy

AS YOU EARN better and become wealthier in the future, you should focus on securing your legacy.

This involves thoughtful plans and strategic decisions. You can consider the following to secure your legacy:

- **Estate Planning:**
  Consult your wealth planner to create a comprehensive estate plan, including wills, trusts, and power of attorney documents.
- **Family Communication:**
  Openly discuss your wealth and intentions with family members, ensuring everyone knows the legacy plan and understands their roles.
- **Education fund:**
  Set up education funds or trusts for future generations, promoting continuous learning and personal development.
- **Family Office:**
  Family offices offer comprehensive services that include

investment management, tax planning, estate planning, philanthropic endeavours and lifestyle management. Consult a good service provider. You can get holistic wealth management as well as customised solutions depending on your needs.

- **Investment in their development:**
  Mentor and guide heirs in financial literacy, business acumen, and ethical decision-making to prepare them for managing wealth responsibly.
- **Documenting Values and Principles:**
  Clearly articulate your values and principles, creating a document that serves as a guide for your heirs in managing the family wealth.
- **Insurance:**
  Consider life insurance policies to provide a financial safety net for your heirs and cover potential estate taxes.

Securing a legacy is not just about finances, it involves imparting values, fostering a sense of responsibility, and making a positive impact on the community and the world.

Instilling values in the family members is crucial. You can even document the family history, stories, and values in written or multimedia formats, ensuring that the legacy extends beyond financial assets to include shared experiences and wisdom.

You must develop and communicate a clear vision for the family's future, emphasising values, principles, and goals that extend beyond immediate financial considerations.

Encourage entrepreneurial endeavours within the family, fostering innovation and wealth creation through new business ventures.

As a wise investor once said, 'True wealth is not just about the size of your bank account; it's about the enduring impact you leave on the world and the values you instilled in those who come after you.'

I'll coclude with the advice—let your legacy be a testament to more than financial success; let it be a beacon of inspiration for generations.

Doctrine 67

Balancing Wealth And Health

ACHIEVING A BALANCE between wealth and health is crucial for our overall well-being. Wealth can provide resources for a comfortable life, but neglecting health can undermine the quality of our life. Here are some insights to understand this better:

- **Physical health:**
  - **Medical expenses:**
    Good health reduces the need for extensive medical expenses. Regular exercise and a healthy diet can prevent lifestyle related disease.
  - **Productivity:**
    Physical well-being enhances productivity, allowing you to make the most of your wealth in both personal and professional pursuits.
- **Mental Health:**
  - **Stress Reduction:**
    Wealth can come with its own set of anxiety and stress.

Prioritising mental health with activities like mindfulness or therapy helps manage stress and maintain focus.
- **Quality of Life:**
  A healthy mind contributes to a better overall quality of life, making your wealth more meaningful.
- **Work-Life Balance:**
  - **Time Management:**
    Balancing wealth and health requires effective time management. Prioritise activities that contribute to both financial success and well-being.
  - **Longevity:**
    Good health increases the likelihood of enjoying the fruits of your labour for a longer time.
- **Social Engagements:**
  - **Community engagement:**
    Allocating time and resources to community or social activities can positively impact mental and emotional well-being.
  - **Networking:**
    Building and maintaining social connections can also be beneficial for both personal and professional growth.
- **Insurance against Uncertainty:**
  - **Health as a Resource:**
    Good health serves as a valuable resource. It acts as a form of insurance, providing resilience in the face of challenges.
- **Long-term Perspective:**
  - **Wealth Sustainability**:
    Chronic health issues can erode financial resources

over time. Maintaining good health ensures that you can enjoy your wealth longer.

In a nutshell, the balance between wealth and health is very important. Prioritising both makes for a more fulfilling and sustainable life. Balancing financial success with physical and mental well-being ensures a comprehensive approach to a prosperous and healthy future. One of the most important factors of wealth creation and preservation is compounding. Time is crucial for compounding to work its wonders and hence life span in terms of number and quality is important to build as well as enjoy wealth.

Doctrine 68

Cultivate A Healthy Relationship With Money

WHEN YOU HAVE enough wealth you should be having a very healthy relationship with money. This can be achieved with mindful practices.

- **This book teaches you to cultivate the habits of:**
  - Savings
  - Strategic and Smart Investment
  - Goal setting with clarity
  - Long-term Approach
  - Discipline and consistency
  - Understand the emotions pertaining to investment, like fear and greed
  - Positive attitude
  - Learning from the rich
  - Take a professional help
  - Gratitude and perspective
  - Purposeful spending
  - Giving back

- Financial literacy
- Balancing lifestyle—money and health
- Financial literacy of family and friends

Integrating all these in your life will help you have a healthy relationship with money. This will enhance not only your life but also the lives of those around you.

When you have money, you should enjoy small things in life. Acknowledging and celebrating the little pleasures of life can help keep you and your money on good terms.

Also, to maintain a healthy relationship with money, you need to cut off financial planning and money matters at times.

Avoid comparisons as it is toxic and spoils your relationship with your money.

As with all relationships, your relationship with money should also evolve with time. Keep it as dynamic and changing as life.

Your relationship with money also depends on your acquisition, spending and management styles. If you have not achieved this balance, then your relationship with the money will be hampered.

Money relationships are also influenced by your beliefs about money. Try to inculcate correct beliefs about money. Know the difference between abundance and scarcity. Adopt an abundance mindset that reduces fear and anxiety which is usually associated with a scarcity mentality.

By addressing both cognitive and emotional aspects, individuals can develop a well-rounded and psychologically healthy relationship with wealth, promoting financial well-being and overall life satisfaction.

Remember, money is not just a number in a bank account; it is a reflection of choices, values, and impact. Cultivate a mindful relationship with wealth where gratitude meets purpose and watch it transform not just your financial landscapes but the very essence of your life.

Doctrine 69

Celebrate The Success

WHEN YOU HAVE enough wealth, you should celebrate your success. Celebrating small wins eggs one on to work towards the larger goal. It reinforces one's belief in oneself and keeps one motivated. This positive reinforcement gives a boost to the confidence, as well.

> 'Our failures are learning for us, but our successes are the fuel that keeps us going. Always celebrate accomplishments, no matter how small. Track your progress so that you can see how far you've come, even if you have not reached your ultimate goal. It will help you stay positive which is the key to continued success.'—Tony Robbins.

But, how do we celebrate? Let's understand this better with some points:
- **Reflect Milestones:**
  Take time to reflect on both personal and professional

milestones. Acknowledging achievements cultivates a sense of accomplishment and gratitude.
- **Express Gratitude:**
Actively recognise and appreciate the factors that contributed to your success. Expressing gratitude fosters a positive mindset and deepens connection with your wealth journey.
- **Share Success with Others:**
Extend the celebrations to those who contributed or supported you. Sharing success builds a sense of community and strengthens relationships.
- **Personal Growth Acknowledgements:**
Recognise personal growth and learning experiences. Understanding your own development fosters self-awareness and resilience.
- **Create Rituals and Recognition:**
Establish rituals or traditions for acknowledging success. Rituals create a sense of ceremony, making achievements more meaningful.
- **Contribute to Others:**
Use success as an opportunity to give back. Contributing to others enhances the impact of success and generates a sense of purpose.
- **Set New Goals:**
Channel the energy from one success into setting new ambitious goals. A continuous pursuit of goals maintains motivation and a forward-looking mindset.
- **Wellness Celebrations:**
Celebrate by investing in personal well-being. Success is holistic and health and self-care is a part of it.

- **Document Your Success Journey:**
  Capture the moments, challenges, and triumphs along the way. It will be a great learning and motivation for the next generation. Documenting the journey provides a tangible reminder of resilience and growth.
- **Host a Get-Together Party :**
  Consider the impact of your success. Recognising positive contributions enhances the meaningfulness of success.

In conclusion, celebrate your accomplishments, no matter big or small. Every win is worthy of a celebration because it is the result of your hardwork. This will keep you focused and contribute to your life satisfaction as you gradually work towards reaching your financial goals.

Doctrine 70

Let's Continue Our Journey Towards Financial Freedom Lifestyle

NOW YOU HAVE enough wealth. Yet, you want to have more. And hence, your journey towards achieving the ultimate FFL continues.

Before moving on to the next phase let's recall some of the significant learnings picked up so far:
- Remember that only passionate and enthusiastic people attract money and keep getting more money.
- You have to create enough net worth for being rich. However, you also need to create enough flow—income and expense—to experience the joys of life.
- Your intellectual wealth should match your financial wealth to keep you wealthy forever. If this is imbalanced then you will lose your wealth.
- Money flow is automatic if you follow the doctrines explained so far, but don't crave to amass wealth all the time. The money flow will follow its pace; welcome it.

- Be transparent and clear on money matters with your children and family; it will forge a good relationship with money.
- If your goals are not based on long-term requirements then your expenses will increase with a double speed than your income does. Set well defined, long-term goals.
- Remember one golden advice from Rockefeller, 'If your only goal is to become rich, you will never achieve it.'
- You have to understand the difference between savings and investing. Team investing with savings to have the effect of power of compounding on your money.
- Acquire as many appreciating assets as possible. This will help you to generate passive income.
- Understand the 3 Musketeers of investment—risk, return and time.
- Never overlook the role of both luck and risk in your journey of wealth creation. Sometimes, a good decision also turns out to be wrong eventually. You have to accept it.
- Both getting money and keeping money require different skill sets and doctrines. Getting money involves risk-taking, hard work, and optimistic decisions. On the other hand, keeping money needs moderate risk-taking, avoidance of greedy attitude, and knowing that nothing is permanent.
- Money can give you financial freedom and that is the highest value for money. Everyone's ultimate goal is financial freedom. With the financial freedom you can do what you want to do, when you want to do, with who you want to do and for as long as you want to do—complete freedom.

- Being rich and being wealthy are two different perspectives. If you are rich, it means you have a high current income. Wealth, however, is not visible; wealth is the money you have that's not spent. Wealth gives you freedom, time and possessions.
- 'What if'—it is the best tool to plan an investment strategy keeping long-term goals in mind.
- You have to be ready to face the volatility and uncertainty that comes with investment strategy. To compound your wealth you have to learn to face volatility, fear, doubt, uncertainty and regret.

So, stride ahead and keep walking in the pursuit of achieving the FFL. Stick to these golden advices and you will not be far from living your FFL.

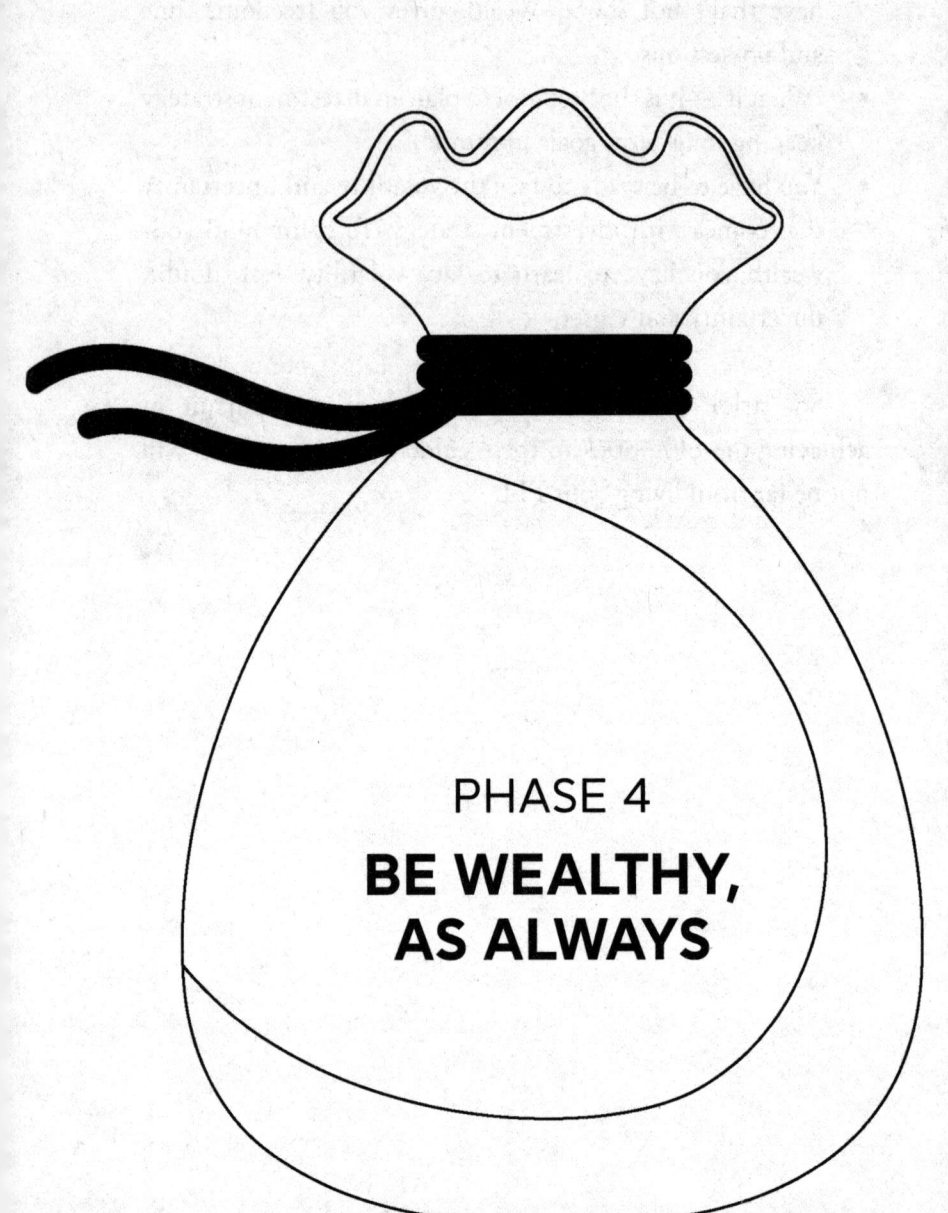

Having acquired wealth, you would want to keep it forever!

So in this section, we will discuss how to keep a hold on your wealth.

As you have got money, you would want to spend it yet maintain your wealth in future.

When you have earned money, you should know how to spend it smartly.

So be ready to start your journey of this phase where you might be walking on the path treaded by the rich and the famous!

Doctrine 71

It's All About Quality

QUALITY SHOPPING IS not about finding the cheapest, but about investing in excellence.

When you are wealthy, you should go for quality shopping focusing on both luxury and value. Go for good quality products and experiences that align with your taste and preference. Prioritise brands with good craftsmanship and durability. Striking a balance between quality and value is crucial. Cost does not equate to excellence. You have to consider your long-term satisfaction and the overall impact of your purchases. You should also try personalised and bespoke options because ultimately it's your money which you should enjoy and experience.

> 'Quality is never an accident; it is always the result of high intention, sincere effort, intelligent direction, and skilful execution.'—William A Foster.

Try to get the combination of quality, convenience and personalisation with your products. If you develop a habit of buying only quality products you can avail advantages like:

- **Durability with Longevity:**
  Quality products are built to last, whether it's clothing, accessories, electronics or any other product. Investing in high-quality products can save your money in the long run.
- **Performance:**
  High-quality products perform better be it reliable electronic products, durable and comfortable clothing or better quality and tasting food and beverages.
- **Aesthetics:**
  Quality products mostly come with superb design and innovative packaging. They are visually appealing and life-enhancing.
- **Resale Value:**
  Quality products are always easy to resale and hence it is always a good investment to buy quality products.
- **Sustainability:**
  High-quality products are mostly made with better materials and manufacturing processes which are mostly environment-friendly.
- **Comfort:**
  Quality products are designed for more comforts and ease so it is always sensible to buy quality products to make your life more convenient.
- **Status and Prestige:**
  Success declares itself with quality products. Quality products are the symbol of status and prestige.

- **Unique and Personalised:**
  High-quality items often offer customised options. They offer unique features and tailor your purchases to specific needs and preferences.

Shopping for quality also depends on your beliefs. In our childhood, many of us were taught:
- Don't spend more than you need to.
- Do not buy expensive things.
- Don't spend too much on your own self.
- It's better to buy ordinary goods on bargain than to buy quality products.

Shopping for quality reflects your personality, thinking and way of living. It shows how you conduct yourself and your business. Overall, buying quality goods always helps you personally and professionally.

Doctrine 72

Don't Be Lazy; Be Very Lazy

IN ONE OF my previous doctrines, I mentioned that lazy people can't create wealth. But when you are wealthy, this principle is applied with a tweak. Remember and follow this principle to hold your investment and protect your wealth:

Don't be lazy; be very lazy.

To protect your wealth and multiply it, you should develop the following qualities:

- Vision to see
- Future Courage to buy
- Patience to Hold

To practise these you have to control your impulse. To control your impulse you need an attitude that is lazy in taking any decision. One of my wealthy clients used to say that to protect wealth, you have to control the impulse to buy or sell.

There may be many rumours in the market, there may be lucrative proposals in the market, but you have to control yourself. Greed and fear—these are the two things you need to learn to control.

To protect and compound your investment you have to control all distractions and attractions. You have to hold your investment with a long-term vision. It is important to find a balance while handling wealth. Being too lazy can lead to missed opportunities; being too active might expose you to unnecessary risks.

There are two type of lazy people—the good ones and the bad ones. You have to be the good one for protecting and multiplying your wealth. The good ones are those who know there are only certain times when the opportunities are available and they have to make the most of it. So, you need not run after each and every opportunities; restrain yourself.

Laziness sometimes acts as a filter that helps you to filter opportunities at your pace. If you apply a certain level of laziness in making investment decisions before buying or selling, then you will find it easier and more convenient to make a correct decision. You train your mind to adopt a style by which you can find better and easier alternatives for everything.

We can call this laziness an active laziness as it holds good for investments by protecting you from getting swayed by big returns. This laziness helps long-term investors to maintain the status quo by avoiding any fresh buy or sell decisions when the market is volatile. In fact, the long-term investors should be too lazy to check the stock prices daily.

Selective inaction or active laziness is a useful trait that helps in attainment of goals and happiness. When you are comfortable with your status quo, goals and investment then you can have enhanced focus for better investment decisions.

Being actively lazy means taking less decisions and hence less chances of wrong decisions. The investment guru, Warren Buffett, used to say that investors should make their investment decisions assuming they will get only twenty opportunities to buy stocks in their lifetime. Selective actions means tremendous discipline in the process.

Our key takeaway here is to read, analyse and gather evidence to get enough confidence to be lazy when needed.

Doctrine 73

Deep Dive Into The Details

BEFORE MAKING ANY purchase, association or contract, check every detail thoroughly.

'Check the small print'—goes the adage. Read the disclaimer and the contract details carefully. Whether it is a contract, policy or an agreement, checking every minor detail is important. Let's deep dive into this and understand the various points of consideration:

- **Terms and Conditions:**
  The fine print contains specific terms and conditions that may not be in the main text. You should check the terms and conditions listed in all your investment policies or agreements and legal documents.
- **Coverage Details:**
  In insurance policies, the fine print often outlines what is covered and what is not. Check the extent of your coverage to ensure your assets and investments are adequately protected.

- **Exclusions and Limitations:**
  Insurance policies, legal agreements, and financial contracts often have limitations and exclusions. Knowing these beforehand is important.
- **Legal Obligations:**
  Know and understand all the legal obligations in the final print. Understand your responsibilities too as failing to adhere to these could harm your wealth.
- **Costs and Fees:**
  All agreements, bank contracts, and financial products often come with associated costs and fees that might not be immediately evident. Hence, before entering into any contracts or agreements be careful about such hidden costs and fees.
- **Right and Responsibilities:**
  The fine print will outline your rights and responsibilities. Knowing what you are entitled to and what is expected of you will help you stay prepared.
- **Risk Factors:**
  Investment agreements and financial products may disclose the potential risks in their fine print. Understanding these risks is crucial for making informed investment decisions that protect your wealth.
- **Legal Recourse:**
  The fine print often details the legal procedures for dispute or conflict resolution, in case any. You should know these procedures in advance.

This is why making a note of every detail mentioned in contracts, agreements and policy is of utmost importance.

Failing to do so can lead to unexpected and financially-significant setbacks that may undermine your wealth protection efforts.

Moreover, always be on the alert for all hidden costs and terms as these can be dangerous.

Make it a habit to read properly, understand diligently and implement carefully with regard to contracts, legal documents and policies.

Small prints may contain the biggest truths. Always read the fine print, for therein lies the essence of understanding and protection.

Remember, humans don't come with written and stated fine prints, so all relationships whether professional, business or personal, need to be observed on the basis of fine words and actions.

Doctrine 74

Spend Only 80 Per Cent Of What You Have

SAVING AND INVESTING a significant portion of your income is a good strategy to build and maintain wealth. It is commonly referred to as the 80:20 rule, where you invest 20 per cent of your income and keep 80 per cent for your expenses. However, the percentage can differ as per your goal, risk appetite and financial situation. But following this 20 per cent rule can give you better financial stability.

There is another wise saying—don't spend it, before you get it. This will also keep your finances in check and regulate your expenses. If you follow responsible spending and budgeting then you can certainly stay wealthy.

There are many benefits of following this rule:
- **Living Within your Means:**
  It teaches you to spend only from what you have, and if you can save or invest at least 20 per cent from what you have then you can have a secured life. Don't ever live on credits or loans; learn to manage living within your means.

- **Budgeting:**
  A detailed budget including a better clarity of your income and planned expenses also can help you curb overspending. Budgeting can help you prioritise essential expenses and meet your saving goals.
- **Emergency Fund:**
  Having an emergency fund is the key to not spending money before having it. Emergency fund is a savings reserve that covers unexpected expenses like medical bills and unforeseen expenses like a car break down etc.
- **Delayed Gratification:**
  If you follow the rule of not spending unless you have the money in hand, it will help you reap delayed gratification. Delaying instant gratification can help you make better financial decisions in the long run.
- **Financial Stress:**
  Depending on the future income for current expenses can create stress, anxiety and financial imbalance. It can lead to a cycle of constantly needing to catch up on bills and debts which can negatively affect your overall well-being.
- **Long-term Goals:**
  Saving and investing for long-term goals, like retirement or a major purchase, is more effective when you plan and save over time rather than relying on your future income.

Remember that buying today against tomorrow's income will incur interest.

Always budget for today and only for today; if you don't have then don't spend—it is as simple as that.

Ask yourself questions like:

- Do I need this urgently, or can I buy it in the future when I have money?
- Is it worthy enough to be bought today against my future income?
- What would be the risks if I invite expenses today against my future income? Is it worth all the risk?
- How will I manage if I spend my future income today and have an unforeseen expense later?

These might look simple and basic, but are difficult to follow.

So, make it a habit to invest at least 20 per cent of your income and avoid buying today against future incomes. Don't mortgage your future for today's desires.

Doctrine 75

Own The Ownership

THINKING LIKE OWNERS, whether as equity owners or business owners, can play a significant role in protecting and growing wealth.

Equity Owners:
- **Diversification and Risk Management:**
  Equity owners often have portfolios with investment in multiple companies or asset classes. Diversifying their investments can help spread risks by restricting the poor performance of an asset class or stock from affecting their overall wealth.
- **Monitoring and Decision-making:**
  By regularly monitoring, the decision of selling and buying can be made based on financial data, market conditions and company-specific performance.
- **Income Generations:**
  An equity owner's thinking is always focused on dividend

paying stocks and long-term appreciations. This provides regular income as well as long-term building of wealth.
- **Compounding Effect:**
Long-term vision builds wealth over time with a compounding effect. Having a long-term vision in a particular company or asset class can help to appreciate investments.

Business Owners:
- **Long-term Vision and Strategy:**
Business owners' vision is always long-term. Their thinking always focuses on sustainability and success over time. This kind of thinking helps in wealth creation.
- **Control over Business Operations:**
Based on their long-term vision, their goals, ethics and principles give them insight into running a company which eventually leads to long-term growth and wealth creation.
- **Tax Planning and Asset Protection:**
These are the essential virtues for the growth of the company over a time against all odds. This thinking can help in protecting and growing wealth.
- **Wealth Diversification:**
Successful business owners often invest their profits in other ventures to diversify risks and to benefit from good opportunities. This helps in growing and protecting wealth.
- **Business Exit:**
When and how to exit from a company requires well thought-out planning. This can be done by selling the existing company or by doing a succession planning. It allows them to extract value from the company in a way that maximises their wealth.

A similar thought process is essential for wealth creation and protection.

Thinking like an owner is a good way of thinking for wealth creation and protection. The investors should think as an owner of their investment corpus and act with the equity owner's or a business owner's mindset. Thinking like an equity owner involves actively managing and diversifying investment portfolios to protect and grow the wealth.

Thinking like a business owner is always based on growing the company in the long run. Both these approaches help in a great way in wealth creation.

The majority of investors have a short-term mindset and that's why they focus on income rather than wealth. Short-term investors have a mindset of timing the market and that's why they have more churning. You cannot time the market but you can time your goal with the business owner-like thinking. It is said that you should never break your compounding engines as it helps create and protect wealth.

In conclusion, thinking like an owner in your investments means taking responsibility for your financial future, making informed decisions and treating your portfolio as a valuable asset to nurture and grow.

Doctrine 76

Preserve For The Old Age

PRESERVING FOR THE old age is like planting a tree and then waiting for the fruits to come so that you can enjoy it. After your retirement in old age, you need more money than you might expect. Let's ponder on some points to understand this:

- **Healthy Lifestyle Choices:**
  One of my acquaintances is a retired gentleman who is now enjoying his life to the fullest. He goes to gym and Yoga classes, practices cycling, plays his favourite games like badminton and table tennis and goes to a club every evening to meet his friends. He believes that these activities keep him fit, healthy and happy. He often goes on short/long trips and keeps himself busy with social and charitable activities. To live such a life you need money, so that when you are retired and have no scheduled activities, you can pursue any recreational activities of your choice.

- **Mental Stimulation:**
  One of my clients had joined music classes to learn piano as an activity to stimulate his mind. He says that he keeps challenging himself by pursuing new hobbies. Lately, he has also joined singing classes. So, in old age, mentally engaging yourself reflects on your happiness and health. So when you retire, keep some money by your side to keep yourself mentally engaged.
- **Social Networking:**
  There are senior citizens clubs which keep senior citizens engaged in social activities. When you meet people and volunteer for a cause, you feel happy and it shows on your overall well-being. These activities keep your emotional threshold on peak which is most needed in old age. All this can be done only when you have a good bank balance in old age.
- **Regular Health Check-Ups:**
  As you age, you have to keep yourself healthy to avoid age-induced sickness and illness. For this you need regular health check-ups which in turn calls for wise financial planning. In your old age, you should be financially independent enough to fund your health expenses.
- **Independence:**
  Financially depending on others in old age is one of the worst situations to face. You cannot ask money from your family or friends. This makes it imperative to plan your finances. At younger age, denial feels more like a sacrifice, but at a later age they bear the brunt as compromise and regret.
- **Giving Back:**
  One of my clients is engaged in animal welfare in his

post-retirement life. He regularly donates to animal shelters and treatment centres as it gives him peace and satisfaction and motivates him to keep going even in old age. He is happy that the money he had invested has now found a good cause.

- **Fulfilling Dreams and Passions:**
  I know a businessman who is enjoying his old age more than any other phase of his life. How, you might be wondering. He goes on long bike journeys and enjoy nature's company, riding his favourite vehicle. He says that he can now follow his passion as he has no responsibilities and can live his life the way he wants. That's absolutely true. If you have enough money with you in your old age then you can follow your passion and live your life the way you want.

In different phases of our life, we have different priorities because of which we cannot live as per our choices. Throughout our life we live for our family, fulfilling our responsibilities. Moreover, most of us start earning enough money after 40. So, the age after 60 is the real time where you have enough time for yourself. Hence, if you have enough money, you can live a good life after 60.

Start keeping some money aside for your old age. For that you can follow some guidelines:

- List down your passion and everything that you want to do after the age of 60. Make a budget to see how much money you will need to pursue your passion and live the life of your dreams after 60. Make this your goal and start investing to achieve that goal.

- Age 60 is a general representation, everyone can decide their own age. It is important to have this age clearly defined and sincerely worked upon.
- If you have failed in investing for old age, then start keeping aside a lump sum to seed your retirement plan.
- You can seek advice from your financial planner for a well thought retirement plan.

Ageing gracefully and maintaining well-being in old age involves healthy lifestyle choices, social and mental engagement, financial planning, pursuing passions, physical and mental health, and giving back to society.

Beware of old age poverty.

Imagine reaching the brink of retirement with a comfortable nest egg, only to face a significant financial setback. It's like being on the verge of winning in Snakes and Ladders, only to land on the snake at 98 and slide back down the board. The frustration and disappointment is immense, as all the progress and hard work seem to vanish in an instant. This scenario underscores the importance of safeguarding your wealth as you approach retirement. Just as a single misstep can undo all your efforts in the game, a major financial loss near retirement can jeopardise your future security and peace of mind.

Starting a game from the beginning is relatively easy; you have the time and energy to rebuild. However, in life, a big financial loss, especially at a later age, is much more challenging. The biggest drawback isn't just the lost money but the lost time and youth. Unlike a game, where you can simply start over, recovering from such a setback in life can be incredibly difficult and time-consuming. Ensuring you have enough money in old age and protecting your accumulated wealth is crucial to avoid such setbacks and enjoy a stable, worry-free retirement.

Remember, investing for old age is not merely a financial endeavour; it is a profound investment in your future well-being, a testament to the life you want to lead in your golden years.

Doctrine 77

The Contingency Fund

MAINTAINING A CONTINGENCY fund is fundamental to sound financial planning. It provides security, peace of mind, and financial flexibility while helping you avoid debt and cope with life's uncertainties. Building and maintaining a contingency fund should be a priority for anyone seeking financial stability and independence.

Just as saving for an old age is important, equally crucial is having a contingency fund. There are many uncertainties in life which can come without warning:

- **Accidents**

    There are accidents which can occur, like vehicle, work related, and industrial among others. You need an emergency fund to sail through the difficult times in case of mishaps that lead to death, or permanent or temporary physical disability of a family member and the resultant financial liability of dependents on us. Loss of assets due to fire can turn out to be a big setback, calling for a large sum of money and resulting into disposing of other productive asset due to lack of liquidity.

- **Illness**
  Medical emergencies, ailments and illnesses often demand lump sum for the treatment.
- **Legal Issues**
  Any legal issues can come knocking, attracting heavy fees.
- **Disputes**
  Land or family and business disputes can be expensive.
- **Natural Calamities**
  Natural calamities like floods, earthquakes, tsunami, or droughts among others can jeopardise your financial stability.
- Recession.
- Liquidation of your business.
- Matrimonial dilutes/dispute with children.

The list can go on and on. You never know what happens in the future. But, how to create a contingency fund?

- Decide upon an ideal amount which can easily provide for financial needs in case of contingencies.
- Identify ideal investment avenue for the said fund. It should be easily encashable and provide return which at least matches the inflation rate post taxation. This is to say the post tax return should at least be equivalent to the average inflation rate so that purchasing power of the money is retained as we do not know when the need will arise. Review and contribute to the contingency fund on a regular basis.

- Use the contingency fund only for the unexpected emergency expenses.
- Replenish the emergency fund after each withdrawal to maintain the size.
- Take relevant insurance policies for covering the emergencies.
- Take advice from your financial advisor to create a sufficient emergency fund.

There is always something coming in a few months that will cost money. So be prepared for the times to come, so that you don't have to spend sleepless nights worrying over covering the costs.

Doctrine 78

Understand Terminal Value Investing

WHEN YOU HAVE created wealth, you want to multiply it. In today's context, the trend in investment is changing fast and value creation from investment has also changed drastically.
Let's understand Terminal Value:
Terminal Value = Intangibles + Megatrends + Leadership
The greatest source of terminal value is the intangibles. In today's time, Soft Assets create more value than Hard Assets.

- **Intangibles:**
  When you invest in a company or a product, try to get complete details on the following intangible points:
- **Culture:**
  Studying the culture of a company before investing in its equity can be valuable. Understanding the company's culture can provide insights into its long-term prospects, management practices and how it treats employees and stakeholders. A strong ethical culture is an indicator of

well managed and sustainable business.

- **Customer Engagement:**
You can predict the future of any company by analysing its customer engagement. Customer satisfaction, retention rate, feedback, and social media presence are the key indicators of any company's future. Strong customer engagement can indicate a healthier business with a potential for growth, while low engagement may be a red flag.

- **Customer Loyalty:**
Customer's loyalty is indeed crucial for a company's future growth. Loyal customers tend to repeat purchases, provide valuable word of mouth marketing, and become brand advocates. Building and maintaining customer loyalty can lead to long-term success and sustainable growth for business. So, before investing in any company's shares, try to know its customer's loyalty.

- **Employee Loyalty:**
Assessing a company's employee loyalty is an important aspect of due diligence before investing. Happy and committed employees often contribute to a company's success and growth. High employee turnover can be a sign of underlying issues within the organisation which could affect its long-term stability and performance. Some of the factors to consider include employee retention rates, job satisfaction, and company's reputation as an employer.

- **Brand:**
Analysing a company's brand is a prudent step before investing. A strong brand can contribute to customer's trust, market position, and long-term success. Analyse

factors such as brand reputation, recognition, consistency, and customer perception. A positive brand image is an asset, while a tarnished reputation may pose risks for your investment.

- **Governance:**
Understanding a company's governance is crucial before making an investment. Key aspects to consider can be its board of directors, executive compensation, transparency, and adherence to corporate governance best practices. Effective governance can help ensure that the company is managed ethically and in the best interests of the shareholders. It is important to review the company's governance structure and policies to make informed investment decisions.

In today's era, any company can grow on its intangible factors compared to its tangible factors like land or buildings and machinery. So, focusing on intangible assets is beneficial in knowing the future prospects of a company. Soft assets or intangible assets give today's companies a hard competitive edge.

However, intangible assets are difficult to value by traditional valuation metrics.

- **Megatrends:**
Another aspect to understand before investing in any category is megatrends.

Megatrends are long-term, global and transformative forces that have a profound impact on economies, industries, societies, and individuals. These trends typically span decades and can shape the world in significant ways. The

following are some of the examples of megatrends:
- Climate changes
- Artificial Intelligence
- Digitisation, (like UPI payments)
- Working Women
- Electrical Vehicles
- Demographic Shifts (Ageing population and Urbanisation)

Understanding and anticipating these megatrends is important for business, policymakers, and investors to adapt and thrive in a changing world.

- **Leadership:**
  Assessing the leadership of a company is a critical aspect of investment analysis. Try and study the following before investing in any company:
  - CEO's track record
  - Management team competence
  - Strategic vision of the company
  - Scale and Innovations
  - Adaptability and Resilience
  - Capital Allocation and Capital Structure
  - Management Depth and Transition

Effective leadership can drive a company's success, while poor leadership can lead to underperformance and risks. All these factors are necessary to study before making an investment decision.

So, understand terminal value investing and the three main pillars involved—intangible assets, megatrends and leadership, for arriving at a good and sound investment decision.

Doctrine 79

Interesting Money Rules

RECENTLY, I CAME across some interesting money rules for savings and investments. I am sharing some of them here since I found them intriguing:

- **50/30/20 Rule:**

One should budget his/her income as per:
- Needs (Food, clothing and housing among others)
- Wants (Vacation, cars, electronic gadgets and other luxuries)
- Goals (Savings, extra debts payments and the like)

  The budget allocation should be:

  Needs = 50 per cent of income

  Wants = 30 per cent of income

  Goals = 20 per cent of income

- **300 Rule:**

Take your current monthly expenses and multiply it by 300.

The resultant amount is what you need to save and invest to maintain your current lifestyle even after retirement.

- **Home Buying Rule:**
  Don't buy a house that costs more than 2.5–3 times your gross annual salary/ income. If the interest rates are high, then this ratio will be 2 times your annual gross income.
- **Rule of 72:**
  You should know by when your investment will double. Follow this simple calculation for this:
  Divide 72 by the growth rate of your investment (expressed as per cent). For example:
  How much time does it take to double your investment at 10 per cent interest? 72 divided by 10=7.2 years
- **20/4/10 Rule:**
  You should follow this rule before deciding to take a car loan. This rule says:
  20 per cent should be the minimum down payment.
  The car should be financed for a minimum of 4 years.
  10 per cent of your gross income should be going toward your car.
  Besides this, always remember that cars depreciate with time.
- **3–6 X Emergency Fund Rule:**
  You must save 3 to 6 months' worth of your basic monthly living expenses as an emergency saving fund.

  This money should be used only for emergencies, such as medical expenses, car damages and the like.
  This fund should be brought out in a savings account and once it is used, try to replenish it again.
- **5–6 X Rule:**
  You should buy term life insurance to protect yourself

and your family worth 5–6 times your gross annual salary/income. However, you should also consider factors like debts and family members to better customise your insurance needs depending on your situation.

- **1 per cent Rule for Impulse Buys:**
  Often, we impulsively buy things we don't need. Follow this practical rule to avoid impulsive buys.
  If the item is over 1 per cent of your annual gross income, wait for at least 3 days before you buy it.
  If you still want the item after 3 days, then go ahead and buy it.

- **The Rule of Automation:**
  Defaults are powerful for savings. At times we get too lazy to save; make savings your default by automating it. The biggest advantage is that your money is saved even before you see or feel it. So try to create an automated money system.

- **Item In, Item Out Rule**
  If you buy one item, then donate or sell another.
  Follow minimalism. Manage both inward and outward possessions to enjoy equilibrium.

These are some of the money saving rules which will help you create and protect your wealth with ease. You can opt for the one that suits you best and follow it with dedication and discipline. These are easier for you to abide by as they create a habit of saving and investing.

Doctrine 80

Teach Your Children How To Create And Protect Wealth

WHEN YOU HAVE ample wealth you want to protect it and pass on to your children. But, can they protect the wealth the way you did? Will your children be able to create more wealth on their own? All these depends on how you educate them about financial literacy.

Teaching financial literacy skills to children is crucial for safeguarding and growing their inheritance. While providing the best education and preparing them for a successful career is important, it is not enough without the knowledge of effective money management. Here's why:

- **Protection of Wealth:** Without financial literacy, children may not understand the importance of budgeting, saving, and investing wisely. This lack of knowledge can lead to poor financial decisions, potentially depleting their inheritance.
- **Growth of Wealth:** Financial literacy equips children with the skills to grow their wealth through informed

investment decisions. Understanding concepts like compound interest, diversification, and risk management can significantly enhance their financial future.
- **Avoiding Debt Traps:** Knowledge of financial management helps children avoid falling into debt traps. They learn to distinguish between good and bad debt, manage credit responsibly, and avoid high-interest loans.
- **Empowerment and Independence:** Financial literacy fosters a sense of empowerment and independence. Children who understand money management are more likely to make confident financial decisions and less likely to rely on others for financial advice.
- **Long-term Planning:** Teaching children about financial planning encourages them to think long-term. They learn the importance of retirement planning, insurance, and estate planning, ensuring they are prepared for future financial challenges.
- **Breaking Conventional Thinking:** The traditional approach of focusing solely on education and career success overlooks the critical aspect of money management. Even high earners can face financial difficulties if they lack the skills to manage their income effectively. Financial literacy bridges this gap, ensuring that children can not only earn money but also manage and grow it wisely.
- **Responsible Wealth Management and Resilience:** Financial literacy encourages children to handle wealth responsibly, and understand the value of money and the importance of ethical financial behaviour. It instils a sense of stewardship, ensuring they use their resources wisely and avoid misuse. Moreover, financial literacy equips them

with the skills to rebuild wealth in case of contingencies. By understanding risk management, emergency funds, and strategic investments, they can recover from significant financial losses and regain their financial footing.

By teaching children these essential skills, you not only protect their inheritance but also empower them to grow and manage their wealth responsibly, ensuring long-term financial stability and resilience.

Create an environment where your children feel comfortable in discussing financial matters and asking questions.

In conclusion, financial education is an ongoing process, and it is important to adapt your teachings to your children's age and understanding. By instilling these insights, you can help them protect and grow their wealth responsibly.

Doctrine 81

What Are You Paying, What Are You Getting?

ALWAYS BE MINDFUL of your financial transactions. Understand what you are paying for and what you are receiving in return as it is the key aspect of maintaining and growing wealth. It involves budgeting, monitoring expenses, and making informed financial decisions to ensure your money is working for you.

The same applies to shopping or buying. In one of our doctrines we discussed buying quality products, but this doesn't mean that you splurge on expensive things which you might get at a reasonable price elsewhere.

There are people who avoid bargaining thinking that the rich never bargain. Contrary to this, the sensible rich would not spend money just because they can. So always make it a habit to bargain.

Remember that spending is easy, but earning is not. We can easily spend the work of years in a few minutes. We have to be cautious and smart when it comes to spending.

We are living in the age of consumerism where there is a constant communication drawing your attention to buy things. They trigger you in all the possible ways. Even when you do not need anything, you fall into the marketing trap and buy without cross-checking or comparing the price.

Try to get a minimum of three quotes, and compare them before buying. Look around to make sure that you are getting the best deal possible. This is what all the sensible and the rich do as they greatly value their hard-earned money.

We should also teach our children the difference between spending and wise spending. Nowadays, the internet makes it easy to compare the prices of everything; use it to the maximum.

If you check and compare the prices before buying, you get the following advantages:
- Cost-efficiency
- Budgetary Control
- Reducing Impulsive Purchases
- Long-term Savings
- Smart Buying
- Balancing between needs and preferences
- Savings
- Money saved is money earned which can be invested

There are multiple benefits of negotiating, checking and comparing prices before buying. This habit empowers you to make informed, cost-effective decisions, ultimately safeguarding and growing your wealth over time.

Before making a purchase, always remember the power of looking around and negotiating. It is not just about saving money; it is about making informed choices and ensuring your hard-earned money goes further.

Doctrine 82

Don't Give Equity

IN THIS ERA of startups and the trend of buying equity, one should be wary of giving equity against the fund required. If you are running a company, you should refrain from diluting your equity.

One should preserve wealth, and just because you are in need of the fund to run the show, you cannot dilute your equity.

Remember a golden advice—a successful businessman will never surrender equity. I know a businessman whose company is doing exceptionally well and so there are people enquiring for equity against a lucrative valuation. Yet, he told them firstly, he doesn't need money and secondly, he is not comfortable being answerable to anyone. Thirdly, if he gets good valuation at all, he has to find out ways to put that money to use.

There is a misconception that a closely held company with all the control in your hand is bad for growth. However, it is not true. Many business advisors and consultants will suggest you to give away equity but with caution. A sensible businessman may borrow and take out loans but he does not give away equity.

Many advisors suggest to clear the bank loans and sell equity so you don't have to pay interest. But an investor takes away many other things with equity, including your peace.

If you ever have to surrender equity then do it against:
- Business skills/expertise
- Strategic alliance
- Complete freedom and hassle-free agreement
- Realistic approach and agreement
- Buy back clause
- Zero voting rights

Moreover, remember to take money only from people who have knowledge of your business and understand it inside out.

When you refrain from giving equity, you retain complete ownership of your company. It means you are not diluting your ownership stake among others, such as investors or employees. Maintaining a higher ownership percentage allows you to have more control over decision-making and a larger share of potential future profits. If preserving wealth and control are your priorities, then alternative methods, like debt financing or bootstrapping might be more suitable. These methods enable you to raise capital without sacrificing a portion of your company's ownership, helping you safeguard your long-term financial interests.

Currently there is a fad of getting the company listed, not for any gains but just as a matter of prestige and the illusion of valuation. Remember, it is not the valuation that brings business growth, it is the business growth that justifies valuation. Listing is crucial for scaling but one needs to do thorough home work and make decisions on the basis of logic and not emotion. Take as much time you want to dilute equity, but never decide in hurry or under pressure.

Final word: guard your equity like a precious treasure; surrender not its value without careful consideration, for in its ownership lies the essence of your journey's worth.

Doctrine 83

Don't Borrow From Friends And Relatives

AT SOME POINT, you might need money for your business and you may find it more convenient to borrow from friends and relatives as they know you and at this phase of wealth they will be more than happy to do so. But, remember, it is not a wise decision. Rather, make them invest into your business. It is always better to encourage relatives and friends to invest in your ventures that align with their financial goals instead of borrowing from them. It not only avoids potential strains on personal relationships, but also allows both parties to benefit from the investment's returns. It fosters a collaborative financial mindset, supporting each other's wealth building endeavours.

Friends and family are not the right sources for funds. It can cause resentments, misunderstandings and suspicions and jeopardise relationships.

There are many reasons to avoid borrowing from friends and family:

- **Strained Relationships:**
  Financial transactions can create tension and suspicion, altering the dynamics of personal connections.
- **Expectations and Pressure:**
  Borrowings come with the package of expectations and pressures that can lead to discomfort or misunderstanding.
- **Lack of Formality:**
  Informal agreements may lack clarity, leading to dispute over repayments.
- **Impact on Personal Dynamics:**
  Financial transactions can affect personal dynamics, potentially causing resentment or unequal power dynamics.
- **Risk to Trust:**
  When repayment faces challenges, it jeopardises trust and strains the relationship.
- **Personal Boundaries:**
  Mixing money with a personal relationship can blur boundaries, impacting both sides emotionally.
- **Point of Misunderstandings:**
  As borrowing from friends and family is casual and not legal or professional, it may lead to misunderstandings.

Instead of borrowing from friends and family, consider alternative financial solutions to maintain clear boundaries and protect the relationships.

I have heard many such cases where borrowing from friends and family led to misunderstandings and emotional strains. Sometimes, it even goes to legal disputes which affect the future generations, too.

In conclusion, bonds with friends and family are priceless. Avoid borrowing; instead encourage shared prosperity through collaborative investments.

Doctrine 84

Go Beyond Wealth

THERE ARE ENDLESS pursuits beyond wealth. True fulfilment comes from meaningful relationships, personal growth, and contribution to the well-being of others.

Knowing when to stop building wealth is subjective; it's essential to balance ambition with contentment and prioritise holistic well-being.

Everything changes with age. When you are at your peak, you should not rest on your laurels. When you have enough wealth, you must enjoy it and share it.

There are many successful businessmen and professionals who retired at the peak of their career and started charitable foundations for the well-being of mankind. When you have accumulated wealth, then you are assured to have a life of compounding interest. So money is not a concern; life goes beyond money.

There are many people who are doing great charitable work. You need not be an influential businessman to do charity; there are many ways to contribute for the well-being of society, environment, education, and poverty among others. You can choose the work which resonates with you the most and contribute with your expertise and knowledge. Being rich is one thing and using your wealth for the well-being of others is another. Practice philanthropy, support local charities, fund educational initiatives, or invest in sustainable projects. You can collaborate with established organisations to start your own initiatives that address specific issues. The key is to use your resources to leave a positive impact and contribute to the betterment of society.

You can use your expertise to offer mentorship, educational programmes, or resources that empower others. You can contribute by financially supporting causes aligned with positive social impact, such as education, healthcare, or environmental conservation. Combining both your knowledge and financial resources allows for a more comprehensive and sustainable contribution to creating better wealth.

You can do innovative pro bono work depending on skills and expertise, like:

- **Legal Tech for Access to Justice:**
  Lawyers and technologists can collaborate to develop innovative legal tech tools that increase access to justice for the underserved populations.
- **Healthcare App for Remote Area:**
  Developers can create a mobile app to provide healthcare information and resources to people in remote or underserved areas, improving health outcomes.
- **Design Thinking Workshops for Nonprofit Organisations:**
  Design or conduct workshops for nonprofit organisations

to help them better understand and address the needs of their target audience.
- **Environmental Conservations through Data Analysis:** Data scientists volunteer to analyse environmental data, helping conservation organisations make more informed decisions about protecting natural resources.
- **Education Gamification for Underprivileged Youth:** Game developers can design educational games to make learning more engaging and accessible for underprivileged children, thereby promoting literacy and numeracy.
- **Social Media Campaigns for Social Causes:** Marketing professionals can create impactful social media campaigns to raise awareness and support for various social issues, leveraging their expertise in communications.
- **Business Strategy Consulting for Nonprofit Organisations:** Business consultants can offer their expertise to nonprofit organisations, helping them develop sustainable business models to achieve their mission more effectively.
- **Pro Bono Architecture for Community Spaces:** Architects and urban planners can contribute their skills to design community spaces, such as parks or recreational areas that enhance the quality of life for residents.
- **Tech Training for Vulnerable Populations:** IT professionals can provide free technology training to vulnerable populations, empowering them with digital skills for better employment opportunities.
- **Cybersecurity Support for Nonprofit Organisations:** Cybersecurity experts can offer pro bono services to

nonprofit organisations to enhance their online security and protect sensitive data.

There are many other avenues which can be explored based on your individual expertise, skills and passion. The world has given you a lot; it's your turn to give it back.

One word of caution—anything you do should not be for fame or social obligation and cultural pressure. Also, it should not be a formality or a stigma that the wealthy need to do charity. Do what you really connect with and believe in, and take its full responsibility right up to the stage of its execution and make a lasting impact.

Just writing a cheque to any NGO or Trust just because you can afford to do so is not charity. I know not one but many so called welfare institutions where the donations are simply wasted with no meaningful impact. I don't blame these institutions; I blame the donors who do not have the time to ensure whether their purpose is served or not.

Pro bono work is a powerful testament to the idea that expertise, when shared selflessly, becomes a catalyst for positive change, forging a path towards a more just and compassionate society.

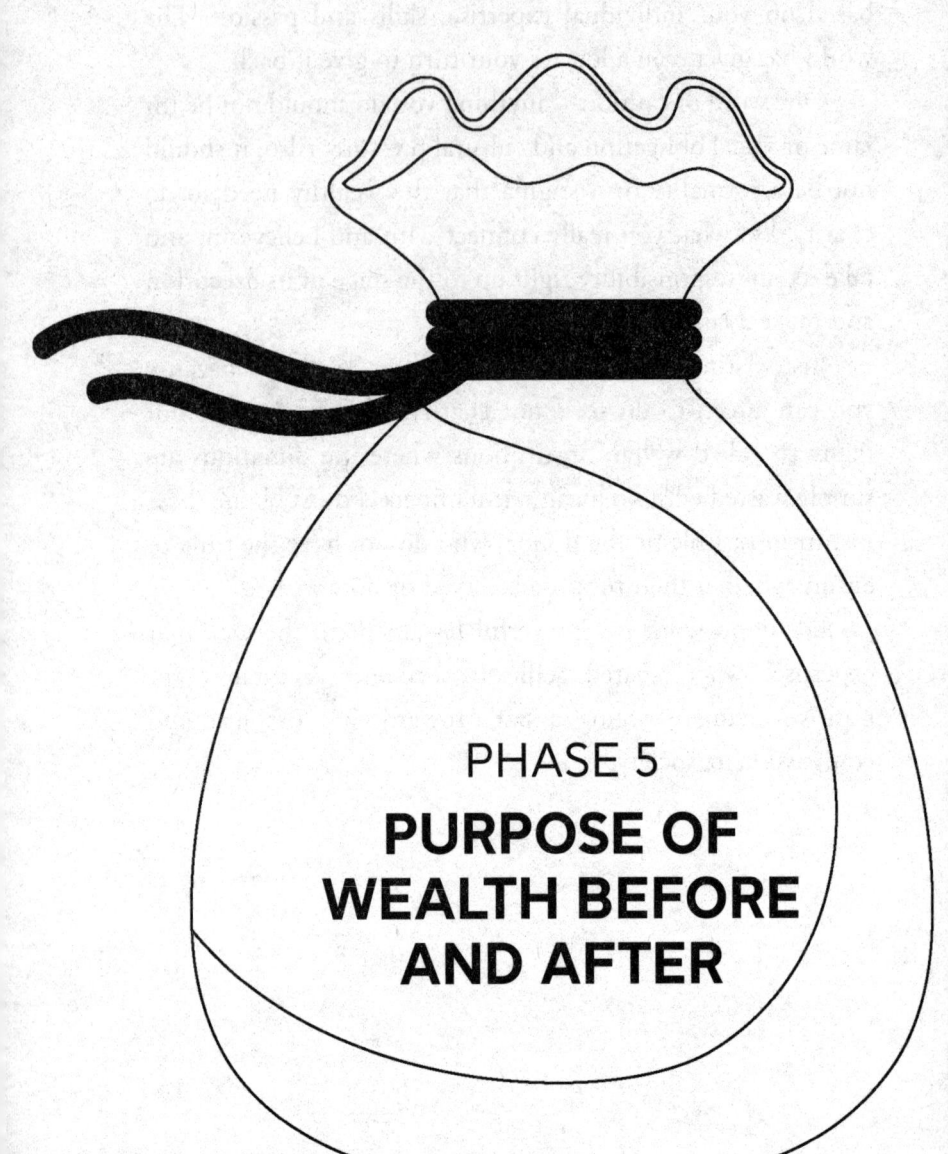

nonprofit organisations to enhance their online security and protect sensitive data.

There are many other avenues which can be explored based on your individual expertise, skills and passion. The world has given you a lot; it's your turn to give it back.

One word of caution—anything you do should not be for fame or social obligation and cultural pressure. Also, it should not be a formality or a stigma that the wealthy need to do charity. Do what you really connect with and believe in, and take its full responsibility right up to the stage of its execution and make a lasting impact.

Just writing a cheque to any NGO or Trust just because you can afford to do so is not charity. I know not one but many so called welfare institutions where the donations are simply wasted with no meaningful impact. I don't blame these institutions; I blame the donors who do not have the time to ensure whether their purpose is served or not.

Pro bono work is a powerful testament to the idea that expertise, when shared selflessly, becomes a catalyst for positive change, forging a path towards a more just and compassionate society.

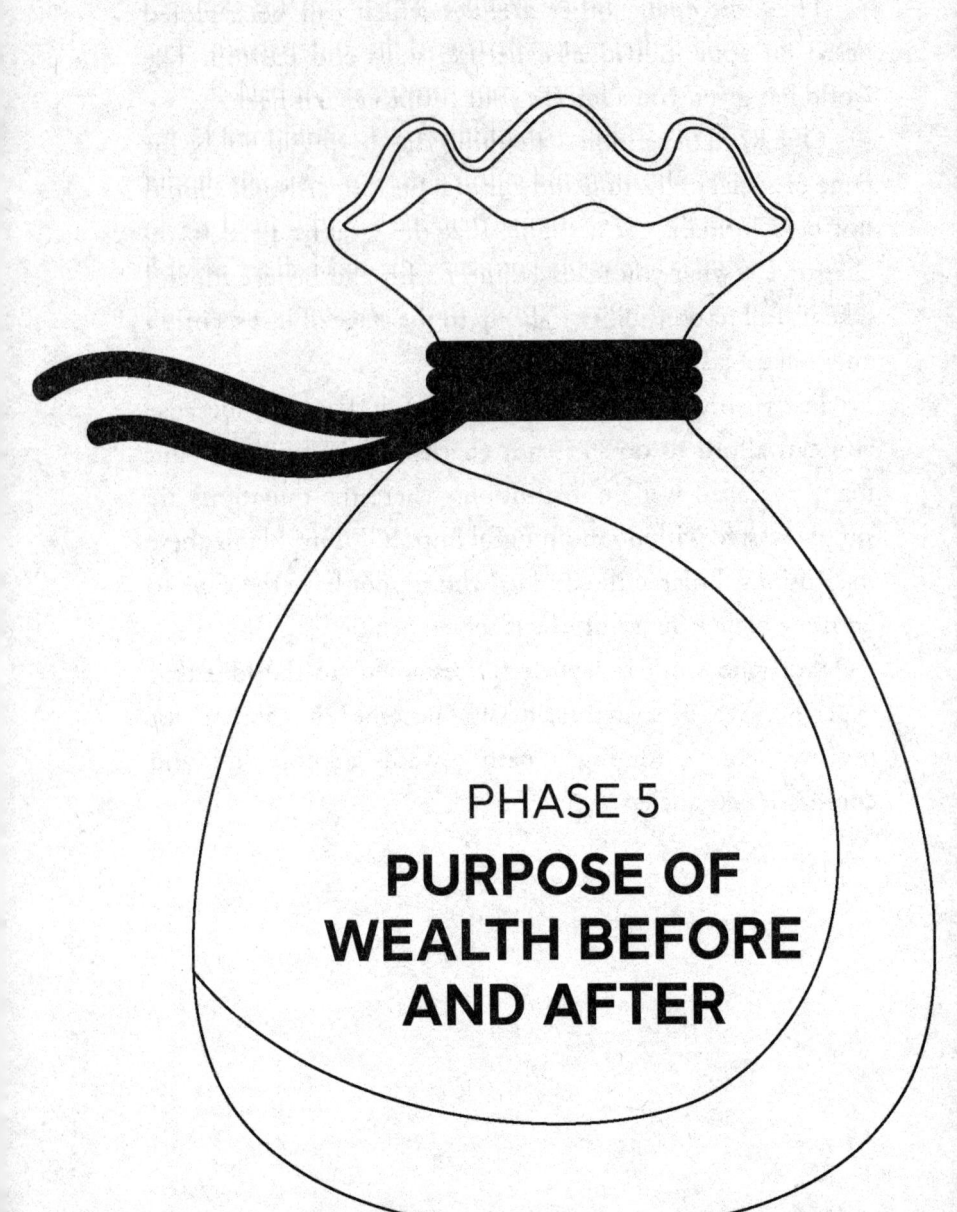

Wealth is like a beautiful painting—you can hang it in your drawing room and look at it, or you can exhibit it, showing people around, so they admire or praise you for that.

When you don't have enough wealth, you strive for it so that you are not deprived of the essentials. So, you work hard, and with all your might and acumen you create wealth. Now what? You cannot take it away with you as you leave the world, or even spend it all alone.

Rightly did someone say:

Money can be earned, grown, guarded, fought over, used well, used badly, won, lost, buried, invested, given away, brought back, exchanged, or divided up. Isn't it amazing? But, the best is to share it.

But, how can you share something you have earned with great efforts? If you share it, will it decrease? Why will you share it with those who are lazy, not focused and don't want to work hard?

Many rich people have shared their wealth since ages. Why do people share their wealth? What is the purpose of wealth when you don't have it and how does it change when you have enough? Wealth is associated with value, intrinsic, tangible as well as intangible.

So let's explore the purpose of wealth and the sharing of wealth.

Doctrine 85

Before Wealth

WEALTH HAS A purpose. Based on your life stage, the definition and purpose of wealth changes. In many traditional societies, the focus was often on communal well-being, subsistence living, and fulfilling basic needs rather than accumulating material wealth.

Human society was primarily a hunter and gatherer community where survival depended on cooperation and resource sharing. As societies progressed, agriculture emerged, allowing for surplus production and the development of trade. However, accumulating material things was not always the primary goal; instead, it often served as a means of ensuring survival and social cohesion.

Religious and philosophical traditions also played a significant role in shaping attitudes towards wealth. Many ancient philosophies, such as Stoicism or Buddhism, emphasised virtues, like wisdom, justice, and compassion over material accumulation.

The shift towards an intensified pursuit of material success gained momentum with the rise of mercantilism, capitalism, and industrialisation. Economic systems evolved, emphasising individual enterprise, innovation, and the accumulation of wealth as markers of success. The shift was accompanied by societal changes that celebrated the pursuit of material success as a reflection of personal achievement and societal progress.

In modern times, the pursuit of material success is often fueled by economic structures, consumerism, and the desire for a higher standard of living. Wealth is now a necessity for the survival and progress of any individual.

Tony Robbins, a renowned author, outlines five levels of wealth crucial for understanding the purpose of wealth. These levels can be compared to Maslow's hierarchy of needs, a psychological theory proposed by Abraham Maslow. Maslow's model is often depicted as a pyramid with five levels, where each level must be satisfied before moving to the next:

- **Physiological Needs**: Basic necessities like food, water, and shelter.
- **Safety Needs**: Security and protection.
- **Love and Belonging**: Social relationships and connections.
- **Esteem**: Respect, self-esteem, and recognition.
- **Self-Actualisation**: Realising personal potential and self-fulfilment.

Let's explore Tony Robbins' five levels of wealth in conjunction with Maslow's hierarchy of needs, considering both material and emotional aspects.
- **Financial Security**

This is the foundational stage where you cover your basic

expenses such as housing, utilities, food, transportation, and insurance. Achieving this level allows you to focus on generating additional income streams, savings, and investments to build wealth. This aligns with Maslow's **Physiological and Safety Needs,** focusing on basic financial stability.

- **Financial Vitality:**
At this level, you have enough money to meet all your basic needs and some additional desires like quality clothing, dining out, vacations, entertainment, and small luxuries. You are now making money and fulfilling extra needs and wants. This corresponds to Maslow's **Love and Belonging,** allowing for social and lifestyle enhancements.

- **Financial Independence:**
Here, you have invested sufficiently to generate wealth, ensuring you no longer need to rely on work or others for financial support. All your needs and occasional luxuries are covered, and the purpose of wealth begins to shift. This relates to Maslow's **Esteem,** providing financial confidence and freedom.

- **Financial Freedom:**
This stage is characterised by having ample money and time to enjoy everything you desire. It represents an ultimate goal where you can fully enjoy life. This also aligns with Maslow's **Esteem,** as it provides a higher level of financial freedom and confidence.

- **Absolute Financial Freedom:**
In this dream scenario, you have an abundance of both money and time. You no longer need to worry about finances and can pursue any interest or passion. At this

stage, the focus of wealth often shifts towards philanthropy. This parallels Maslow's **Self-Actualisation,** where wealth enables pursuing passions and philanthropy.

So you have to level up and aim to reach the Absolute Financial Freedom life.

Your purpose for wealth evolves at each level. Initially, the focus is on fulfilling basic needs. As you progress, you enhance your lifestyle, enjoy occasional luxuries, and eventually pursue personal interests and hobbies. Ultimately, you may shift towards philanthropy and making a positive impact. Throughout this journey, it's crucial to maintain a focus on wealth creation, ensuring it isn't overshadowed by comfort and luxury. Wealth is the ultimate source of freedom, while comforts and luxuries are the means to a more enjoyable journey. Progress should be structured, with a consistent focus on wealth creation, preservation, and transfer, avoiding the temptation to skip levels or act beyond your current stage. Everything changes when wealth becomes freedom. Freedom is what we all want. So, wealth creation is a journey, and the purpose of the wealth changes as per the level of wealth. You have to enjoy every bit of your journey and understand the purpose of wealth.

The true purpose of wealth lies not merely in its accumulation, but in its conscientious deployment to uplift lives, foster compassion, and contribute meaningfully to the well-being of both individuals and society.

Doctrine 86

After Wealth

WEALTH IS ALWAYS integrated with purpose. Wealth accumulated without purpose has no meaning and can hardly be sustained or enjoyed. Most of us, including me, who come from middle class families, think that success means tons of money.

But when wealth lacks purpose, it makes you unhappy. There are five pillars for lasting happiness:
- Wealth
- Purpose
- Health and Longevity
- Legacy
- Experience

These five pillars are integrated with each other. A certain amount of money is essential to live a life of freedom. But, you also need to find a purpose in life, as without it the inner peace cannot be found.

Pursuing wealth is often accompanied by a desire to give back and integrate purpose into one's financial success. Let's break down the journey of wealth:

- **Accumulating Wealth:**
  The initial phase is to accumulate wealth through various means, such as business ventures, investments, or a successful career.
- **Values and Purpose:**
  At one stage in your life, you thrive on values and purpose beyond material success. This introspection can lead to a desire to contribute positively to society.
- **Philanthropy and Giving Back:**
  Giving back involves sharing one's wealth with charitable causes or initiatives that align with personal values. It can be any social cause, like supporting education, health care, or environmental conservation among others.
- **Social Entrepreneurship:**
  Some individuals choose to integrate purpose directly into their wealth creation by pursuing social entrepreneurship. This involves establishing businesses that have a positive impact on society while generating profits.
- **Impact Investing:**
  Here individuals intentionally invest in projects, companies, or funds that aim to generate both financial returns and measurable positive social or environmental impact.
- **Corporate Social Responsibility (CSR):**
  Those involved in business can integrate purpose into wealth by implementing CSR practices. With this the larger impact on society and environment can be generated.

- **Building Sustainable Practices:**
  Wealth with purpose often involves adopting sustainable practices in both personal and professional spheres. This can involve environmentally friendly choices, ethical business practices, and opportunities.
- **Education and Empowerment:**
  Community upliftment can be achieved with this by giving access to knowledge, skills, and opportunities.
- **Long-term Commitment:**
  Integrating purpose into wealth is a long-term commitment. It requires ongoing reflections, adaptation, and a genuine dedication to make a positive impact beyond financial contribution.

The journey from wealth accumulation to integrating purpose involves a conscious shift from personal success to contributing to the well-being of others.

Future trends suggest a growing emphasis on impact investing where individuals seek both financial returns and positive social or environmental outcomes.

Philanthropy is likely to incline towards more strategic and collaborative efforts, leveraging technology for effective giving and measurable impact. CSR and sustainable business practices are expected to become integral parts of wealth management strategies.

When you have wealth, you have to keep abreast with the future trends of wealth and giving back:
- Increasing interest in aligning investments with personal values led to a surge in impact investing. Sustainability, clean energy, and social progress are trending.

- The use of data analytics, blockchain, and other technologies for more informed and traceable philanthropic efforts. Donors may increasingly demand measurable outcomes and transparency in the use of their contributions.
- As wealth is passed on to the younger generations, there is a growing expectation for these heirs to engage in purposeful and socially responsible investing.

Family, offices and wealth advisors may play a crucial role in educating and guiding the next generation toward impactful giving.

In essence, the relationship between wealth and giving back reflects a growing awareness that financial success comes with a responsibility to contribute positively to the well-being of others and the planet. Integrating these aspects leads to a more fulfilling and purpose driven approach to both wealth creation and social impact.

Doctrine 87

Become Wealth Wise

HAVE YOU HEARD of the famous Bollywood star Bhagwan Dada, who is known for his unique dancing style and a movie called *Albela*? He was so talented that he reached at the peak of the Indian film industry. He made films where he did everything—from designing costumes to arranging meals for the cast. He had a 25-room waterfront bungalow at Juhu and a fleet of 7 imported cars, which he used to take for each day of the week. But, he didn't plan his wealth well and spent his final years in a chawl of Mumbai.

There are many other examples with one common lesson—those who abuse their wealth don't stay wealthy for long.

One gets wealthy with talent, opportunities, hard and smart work. But loses it due to a lack of planning and abuse of wealth. Let's take a deep dive and answer some questions:
- Why do we get wealthy?
- What is the best use of wealth?

- What are your wealth related goals—short, medium and long-term?
- What will you get along with the wealth?
- Are you ready to share your wealth?
- How would you like to see yourself after having wealth?
- When you die wealthy, how would you like to be remembered?
- What legacy do you want to leave behind?

Once you are wealthy, it becomes imperative for you to teach your children the value of money—how to earn, use, save, invest money, and, most importantly, how to use wealth wisely. Children should be taught about tax, insurance, and responsible behaviour with money. No schools or institutes are teaching this, and that's the basic problem we all are facing as far as wealth management is concerned.

Throughout our journey, we have learnt about all aspects of earning and managing wealth. We have also discussed the changes in thought process and responsibilities both before and after wealth. But, the basic, and the most important, thing is to use wealth wisely, and to teach your family and children about using wealth wisely.

Finally, true wealth is not just measured in currency, but in the judicious use of resources to enrich lives, uplift communities, and leave a legacy of positive impact for generations to come.

Doctrine 88

Explain Poverty To Children

IF YOU HAVE enough wealth, then be careful before giving money to your children easily. A monthly allowance is a good idea, but don't be too generous; you should be strict about giving away the money.

Children should know the value for money right from the beginning. They should know the importance of savings, investments and wealth creation. They should be taught budgeting, setting goals and using money judiciously. They should also know the darker side of misusing money, like sex, drugs, bad company and things that can harm them.

Your children should not take money matters lightly. They should understand how to earn and respect money. They should know how to set some money aside for buying their future house or may be starting a business. All these points are pertinent and need adequate planning.

Your children should know and experience poverty if they want to value money. When dealing with children, the topic of poverty should be approached with sensitivity. You can explain that poverty means when some families don't have enough money for basic needs like food, clothing, or shelter. Make them understand the emotion of empathy and the importance of helping others. Explore volunteering opportunities or engage in simple acts of kindness to foster compassion and understanding in kids. There is a huge difference between sympathy and empathy. Teach them empathy.

Making kids understand or experience poverty can be challenging, but you can come up with activities to help children understand better. Begin with a discussion about local food, clothing, and shelter. One of my clients did exactly this. Let's explore some similar activities which might help.

- **Food Scarcity:**
  Go to a remote place and spend time with the underprivileged. Have a meal with them where the portions are smaller or the dishes are not as varied, explaining that some families cannot afford regular nutritious meals.
- **Limited Resources:**
  Set a budget for a day and let them experience making choices within the budget, discussing how it reflects the decisions underprivileged families often face. You can make it for a month or holiday on a limited budget. It is not a one-time activity. It needs to be engraved in family routine and value system. There is no one-size-fits-all approach; experiment and try to find what suits your family.
- **Living Conditions:**
  They can visit people living in huts or smaller homes. Try to temporarily simplify their living conditions. Discuss

what it might be like to share a smaller home or to lack some basic amenities.
- **Community Awareness:**
Visit local charities or community centres that support those in need. It helps children see the impact of poverty and learn how they can make a positive difference.
- **Second-hand Shopping:**
Take them to second-hand stores to shop for clothing. Explain that some families rely on these options due to financial constraints.

One of the biggest mistake people commit in the name of teaching value for money is linking academic success to monetary benefits and making children earn their pocket money by doing chores. By this you are just teaching them trading and self-centric behaviour, viz 'what is there for me' or 'what is my benefit'.

Children should understand that doing household work and helping family members is their responsibility and cannot be measured in monetary terms. Similarly, academics is for their overall development to cultivate a learning mindset, build relationships and network. Education is not just about marks and degree, but important for overall personal development in terms of social skills and a fertile mindset which is always open to learn new things.

With larger wealth people either tend to go overboard in terms of children's education or become too casual about the same.

Throughout these activities, emphasise empathy, understanding, and the importance of helping others. Discuss the systematic issues contributing to poverty while reinforcing the idea that everyone deserves dignity and compassion.

Teaching children about poverty is not just about weaving words, but about crafting experiences that open their hearts to empathy. In the tapestry of understanding, we weave threads of compassion, kindness, and the shared responsibility to make our world a place where no one is left behind.

Doctrine 89

Choose Charities Wisely

WHEN YOU HAVE money, you will get many requests and direct approaches for making donations. There are many charities and other similar entities working, but which of these are genuine? You have to choose your charity smartly.

Ask some simple questions before deciding on your charitable activity. Here are some tips:
- Decide which cause is important for you—saving the planet, serving the underprivileged, catering to the children, contributing to education and literacy, solving health issues or anything else.
- How do you want to contribute, monetarily or manually? Do you want to help people as an advisor? Or, do you want to volunteer and help them raise funds?
- Check the track record of the charities you want to be involved with. Do this diligently and decide if your ideals align with theirs.

Trust your gut feeling. Choosing a charity or good cause involves a thoughtful process. Here is the detailed guidelines:
- **Define your Values and Interest:** Identify the causes that matter to you the most. It may be education, health, environment, poverty or any other issues. Understanding your values and interests will help you narrow down the options.
- **Conduct a Research:** Look for reputed organisations working for your chosen cause. Utilise online resources, such as websites, articles, and social media handles to find organisations that align with your values.
- **Assess Transparency:** Check if the organisation is transparent about its activities, goals, and finances. Reliable charities provide detailed information on how they use donations, their activities and the impact they generate.
- **Evaluate Impact:** Access the effectiveness of the organisation's programme. Look for evidence of tangible outcomes and positive changes in the communities they serve. Impact reports, case studies, and success stories can provide insight.
- **Financial Accountability:** Examine the organisation's financial health. For this you can check the various resources available.
- **Check for Endorsement:** Explore endorsements or partnerships with other reputed entities. Collaborations with well-known institutions or recognitions from experts in the field can be indicators of credibility.
- **Reviews and Ratings:** Check all reviews and ratings across the field—from donors, volunteers, and independent

evaluators. This will help you make a decision.
- **Local Impact:** Choose local charities which directly impact your community. Local organisations always have a deep understanding of local issues and can make a significant difference at the grassroots level.
- **Long-term Commitment:** Assess the organisation's vision to long-term solutions. Sustainable initiatives and focus on grassroot causes of issues can have a lasting impact. Choose the charities which have a long-term agenda.
- **Diversify Your Giving:** Try to diversify your giving. By this you can cover more issues and reduce the risk of some charities failing to deliver.

Choosing a charity or a cause is your personal decision but the thorough research will surely help you put your money to good use.

Remember, selecting a good charity is not just about giving, but about investing in the positive change you wish to see in the world. Research, transparency, and alignment with your values turn compassion into impactful action.

Trust your gut feeling. Choosing a charity or good cause involves a thoughtful process. Here is the detailed guidelines:
- **Define your Values and Interest:** Identify the causes that matter to you the most. It may be education, health, environment, poverty or any other issues. Understanding your values and interests will help you narrow down the options.
- **Conduct a Research:** Look for reputed organisations working for your chosen cause. Utilise online resources, such as websites, articles, and social media handles to find organisations that align with your values.
- **Assess Transparency:** Check if the organisation is transparent about its activities, goals, and finances. Reliable charities provide detailed information on how they use donations, their activities and the impact they generate.
- **Evaluate Impact:** Access the effectiveness of the organisation's programme. Look for evidence of tangible outcomes and positive changes in the communities they serve. Impact reports, case studies, and success stories can provide insight.
- **Financial Accountability:** Examine the organisation's financial health. For this you can check the various resources available.
- **Check for Endorsement:** Explore endorsements or partnerships with other reputed entities. Collaborations with well-known institutions or recognitions from experts in the field can be indicators of credibility.
- **Reviews and Ratings:** Check all reviews and ratings across the field—from donors, volunteers, and independent

evaluators. This will help you make a decision.
- **Local Impact:** Choose local charities which directly impact your community. Local organisations always have a deep understanding of local issues and can make a significant difference at the grassroots level.
- **Long-term Commitment:** Assess the organisation's vision to long-term solutions. Sustainable initiatives and focus on grassroot causes of issues can have a lasting impact. Choose the charities which have a long-term agenda.
- **Diversify Your Giving:** Try to diversify your giving. By this you can cover more issues and reduce the risk of some charities failing to deliver.

Choosing a charity or a cause is your personal decision but the thorough research will surely help you put your money to good use.

Remember, selecting a good charity is not just about giving, but about investing in the positive change you wish to see in the world. Research, transparency, and alignment with your values turn compassion into impactful action.

Doctrine 90

Spend Your Money Wisely

WE ARE ALWAYS cautious about spending our own money. But, when we have enough money it is difficult to spend it all by ourselves. You have to hand it over to others for various purposes. Though it is risky, it is often essential, too.

When you run an organisation, you delegate tasks and your money has to be managed by others. But you have to be cautious. You have to keep a regular check on everything. I have noticed that the rich and successful people hardly hand over anything entirely.

I know a businessman who has an agent to buy all his equipment. The businessman merely used to sign the cheques while the agent took care of all the other work. No wonder, the agent was soon driving a new posh car. There is nothing bad about delegating work but in money matters, you should know where your money is going.

Many of us do exactly the same thing. For example, I used to buy electronics without visiting the showroom or checking the deal. I had an agent whom I depended on for everything related to electronics. But then I realised that I should check all the deals before buying anything.

It is often said that you have to control your expenses if you want to control your finances. With uncontrolled expenses you lose control on your finances which eventually results in losing your dignity.

Never give blank cheques to anybody. Nor should you give anyone the authority to sign cheques on your behalf. At times you may have to assign a signing authority, especially in business and sometimes in personal finances, too. While doing so, devise proper internal controls and processes to minimise the risk of deceit or human errors and keep a watchful eye. 'Fill it, shut it, forget it' only work in an advertisement campaign and not in personal finances. Don't hand over credit cards to anybody. Do not keep a joint account. Before spending, check the small print. Check everything, question everything. Stay in control always. One word of caution—do not overdo it or be obsessed about it; maintain a balance.

The principle of not letting others spend your money on your behalf emphasises the importance of personal financial responsibility and decision-making. Let's see how:

- **Autonomy and Accountability:**
  - Taking charge of your finances ensures that you have control over how your money is used.
  - It gives you the sense of accountability, as you are directly responsible for the consequences of your financial decisions.
- **Alignment with Personal Goals:**
  - It is only you who know and understand your financial

goals and its importance. Don't expect others to know it as well as you do.
- o Direct involvement allows you to align spending with your specific objectives, like savings, investments, buying a home, education or retirement etc.
- **Risk Management:**
  - o Entrusting someone to spend on your behalf may expose you to risks, such as potential misuse or mismanagement of funds.
  - o Personal involvement enables you to assess and mitigate risks according to your own risk tolerance.
- **Informed Decision-Making:**
  - o Being actively involved in financial decisions requires knowledge and understanding of your financial situation.
  - o It encourages informed decision-making based on your financial literacy and awareness.
- **Avoidance of Exploitation:**
  - o Allowing others to spend on your behalf may expose you to potential exploitation or manipulation.
  - o Maintaining control safeguards against financial abuse or undue influences.
- **Flexibility and Adaptability:**
  - o Financial situations change, and personal circumstances evolve.
  - o Having control over your finances allows you to adapt spending patterns according to the changing needs and priorities.
- **Empowerment and Confidence:**
  - o Taking control of your finances empowers you to be

confident and gives you choices of informed decisions.
- It builds financial confidence and a sense of empowerment in managing your economic well-being.
- **Personal Growth and Learning:**
  - Direct involvement in financial matters provides opportunities for personal growth and learning.
  - Overcoming challenges and making decisions enhances financial literacy and resilience.
- **Preventing Unwanted Obligations:**
  - Allowing others to spend on your behalf might lead to commitments or obligations that you might not like to take on.
  - Maintaining control ensures that financial commitments align with your intentions and plans.
- **Long-Term Financial Stability:**
  - Direct involvement in your spending gives you financial stability.
  - It allows you to save, invest and plan your debt management as per your financial goals.

By adhering to the principle of not letting others spend your money on your behalf, you retain control, mitigate risks, and ensure that your financial decisions align with your unique aspirations and circumstances.

In essence, guard your wallet as you would your dreams; never let others spend your money, for in financial autonomy, you find the key to shaping your own destiny.

Doctrine 91

Don't Lend Money To Friends And Family

SHARING YOUR WEALTH and lending your money are two different things. If you lend money to your friends and relatives, be prepared to lose both your money as well as the relations. If you are ready to write it off then only you should lend them money. The relationship will be affected if you expect them to return it but they fail to do so.

There is a difference between sharing wealth and lending money.

Sharing of Wealth
- **Voluntary and Generous:**
  Sharing of wealth involves willingly giving a portion of your resources, whether it's money, possessions, or opportunities, without expecting a direct repayment.
- **No Expectation of Return:**
  Unlike lending money, there is typically no expectation from the receiver to return the shared wealth. It is a one-

way transfer based on generosity or a desire to help others.
- **Altruistic Motives:**
The motivation for sharing wealth is often altruistic, driven by a genuine desire to leave a positive impact or contribute to the well-being of others.
- **Less Formal:**
Sharing is often informal and doesn't involve detailed agreements or repayment plans. It can be spontaneous and based on personal relationships or a sense of community.

Lending Money

- **Transaction with Expectation:**
Lending money involves a financial transaction with the expectation that the borrower will repay the amount within a specified time frame and under agreed upon terms.
- **Mutual Agreement:**
There is a formal agreement or understanding between the lender and borrower, outlining the terms of the loan, including the repayment schedule, interest, if any, and consequences for non-repayment.
- **Financial Transaction:**
Lending is a financial transaction driven by the expectation of getting the money back. Often, it is more business-like in nature, involving clear terms and conditions.
- **Potential Strain on Relationships:**
Due to the formal nature of lending, there is a higher risk of straining personal relationships, especially if the borrower faces a situation of non-payment.

I'll conclude with one golden rule that must be followed—preserving relationships is priceless; never lend money to friends and relatives, for the cost of strained ties can far exceed any borrowed sum.

Doctrine 92

Don't Lend; Buy Equities

WHEN YOU ARE rich, people approach you for loans, joint ventures, partnerships and all sorts of business proposals. Even your relatives and friends will approach you for favours. Your family will also ask you for loans. After all, everybody needs money.

So, what will you do whenever someone asks you for money?
- No
- Yes
- Let me think
- Will take equity
- Will give against collateral guarantee
- Will give a convertible loan

Let me answer this for you—don't lend money (if possible). Alternatively, you can take equity or give a convertible loan.

However, taking equity is the best option. The borrower is taking money for the business, and how the business fares in the future is unknown.

Lending typically involves providing funds to others with the expectation of getting the principal back along with the interest. However, this strategy suggests investing in stocks rather than lending.

Equities represent ownership in a company, and their value can appreciate over time, potentially offering higher returns than the interest gained from lending. This strategy aligns with the idea of participating in the growth of business which can lead to capital gains as the value of the stocks increases.

It is important to note that investing in equities has its fair share of risks as the stock market can be volatile. Unlike lending, where you receive a fixed interest, the value of equities can fluctuate. This strategy assumes a willingness to accept market risks in pursuit of potentially higher returns compared to traditional lending. Always consider your risk tolerance and financial goals before implementing such strategies.

There are many advantages of taking equities like:
- Shared Success
- Long-term Commitment
- Risk Mitigation
- Motivated Collaboration
- Adaptability in Repayment
- Potential for Higher Returns
- Tax Advantages

However, the advantages can vary based on the specific context and the nature of the business.

Remember that rather than lending, consider taking equity—a partnership in growth where success is shared and commitment aligns with shared prosperity.

Doctrine 93

Bonding Of Wealth

WE ALL KNOW this universal truth—you come on earth empty-handed and you go from here empty-handed. You can't take anything with you when you die. Despite knowing this, it is difficult to get rid of the wealth bondage.

So, what will you do after amassing all the wealth? How do you plan to leave it behind? These are two relevant points to ponder upon.

Material wealth and possessions have no bearing on one's afterlife or ultimate existence. Let's understand this better:

- **Temporal Nature of Life:**
  In a philosophical sense, life is seen as a transient journey, and material possessions are viewed as trivial and inconsequential in the grand scheme of existence.
- **Mortality and Impermanence:**
  The inevitable death underscores the impermanence of material wealth. Any financial success or accumulation of possessions has to be left behind when you die.

- **Philosophical and Spiritual Perspective:**
  Various religious and philosophical traditions advocate the importance of spiritual values and virtues over material wealth. Wealth is indeed essential and necessary but the true essence of a person transcends their earthly possessions, and, hence, the focus should be on spiritual growth and moral development.
- **Legacy Through Actions:**
  The impact of one's actions, kindness, and contributions to society can leave a lasting legacy.
- **Prioritising Experiences:**
  Experiences, relationships, and personal growth hold more significance than the accumulation of material wealth. Memories and connections forged during one's lifetime are considered more enduring and meaningful.
- **Detachment from Materialism:**
  Embracing a minimalist or mindful approach to possessions can lead to a greater focus on what brings genuine fulfilment and happiness.
- **Philanthropy and Giving Back:**
  Recognising that wealth has limited utility after death, some individuals choose to engage in philanthropy and charitable activities during their lifetime.
- **Focus on Inner Well-being:**
  Many religions emphasise inner fulfilment, personal growth, and meaningful relationships.

The transient nature of life encourages individuals to contemplate the true meaning and purpose of their existence beyond the acquisition of material wealth.

However, you should plan on choosing a deserving successor to take care of your wealth. You have to calculate your tax liability and other finances. However, this is something that your financial and legal advisors would look into.

In short, you should focus on sharing and giving back. Death is the ultimate equaliser; in the end, the wealth we amass in life remains behind as we embark on our final journey empty-handed.

Doctrine 94

Be Assertive When You Are Wealthy

WEALTHY PEOPLE ARE the easiest targets; be careful. People will come to you with all sorts of proposals and offerings like:

- Low interest loans
- High interest investments
- Double your money in the shortest span
- You might be owing something, they know you since long
- Memberships
- Trusteeship

It is difficult to find out the genuine from the fake. So you have to be alert all the time. Bombarded with so many proposals, how do you decide when to say yes and when to say no, or both?

Saying no to friends and family will be easy when you follow our doctrine—not to lend money to friends and family. So they already know this and so will not ask again.

Saying no in business is also easy as you can always say that you have to ask your accountant or business advisor. This will help you to buy time, and by putting in another interface in between the communication will not be easy the next time. In case the offer is genuine, you can always discuss it directly. So, let's see when to say yes or no:

- Say no if your gut feeling says so.
- If the proposal is verbal and without any presentation or documentation and proof, say no.
- Always say no to strangers.
- Never be ashamed or feel guilty of denying anything. It is your money and you can do whatever you want to.
- Don't feel guilty when saying no.
- Understand the proposal clearly.
- You should know what is being asked for.
- Always take advice of an expert.
- Keep a close-door policy; create an interface; don't meet people easily.
- Avoid saying yes only to please people; they might emotionally blackmail you.
- Always be clear when saying no.
- Be assertive to guard your wealth.
- Do not commit to anyone.
- Know who you are dealing with; do not offend the wrong person.
- Despise free lunches.

In conclusion, saying no is about setting boundaries, making strategic decisions, and prioritising what truly matters to you. It is a crucial skill for maintaining both your financial health and overall well-being. Assertiveness is the guardian of wealth; confidently protect what you have earned to ensure its lasting prosperity.

Doctrine 95

Give With No Strings Attached

IF YOU CAN give them money without any things attached to it, you are doing well.

Have you ever tried to give money to those, who
- Have not asked for it?
- Do not need it?
- Deserve it?
- Will use it wisely?

And if yes, have you been able to give them money without making them feel indebted to you? If you are able to do it, it is best as you find them without any strings attached.

There are ways to give your money without them feeling guilty or embarrassed:
- You can ask them to pay back when they win a jackpot or a lottery.
- Ask them to pay back when they have enough.
- Tell them you want to see them happy.

- Mention it as one of the friendship duties.
- Tell them that you feel happy by giving them.

There are many other creative ways in which you can give your money for a good purpose. You can also try:
- Giving unconditional gifts. This involves providing funds to individuals or organisations without specifying any conditions or requirements for how the money should be used.
- You can communicate clearly that the money given is a gift and there are no expectations of repayment or specific actions in return. Transparency about your intention to offer unconditional support helps ensure the recipient understands the nature of the gift.
- Additionally, consider respecting the recipient's autonomy by allowing them the freedom to use the funds in a way that aligns with their needs or goals.

To give money without making someone feel embarrassed, you have to approach the situation with sensitivity and respect. You can consider the following approach, too:

- **Choose the Right Settings:**

  Find a private and comfortable setting to discuss the gift, allowing the recipient to feel at ease without the fear of judgement.

- **Express Genuine Concerns:**

  Frame the conversation with genuine concern for their well-being and offer support.

- **Mutual Benefit:**

  Explain them what you get by doing that and what difference money can make for him.

- **Positive Attitude and Communication:**
Use positivity focusing on how the gift can help him in future.
- **Privacy:**
Respect their privacy by not disclosing the gift to others without their permission. This helps prevent potential embarrassment.
- **Offer Anonymity:**
Provide the gift anonymously to help the recipient accept it gracefully.
- **Provide Options:**
Offer the gift in a way that allows them to maintain their dignity. You can offer it as a gesture of friendship rather than charity.

Remember, always be empathetic and understanding of the other person's feelings, and be prepared to respect their decision even if they decline the offer. By giving anonymously, you illuminate lives without casting shadows, allowing your kindness to speak louder than your name ever could.

Doctrine 96

Take Advice From Those Who Take Responsibility

OFTEN, ADVICE COMES free, and that's why, without responsibilities. Many advisors charge money for the advice, but do they take responsibility for their advice? If not, then don't accept them.

While appointing an advisor, know the following:
- What are your expectations from him?
- Why do you need advice?
- Prepare a clear road map; what do you want to achieve with the help of the advisor?
- Scope of work for the advisor is to be described and agreed upon mutually
- If the advisor fails to deliver, then what actions should be taken?
- Clearly define various options, like Plan A, Plan B

Appointing an advisor is a two-way sword, so appoint them only after having a complete clarity.

Moreover, remember that nobody can make you rich. For reaching that stage, you have to work hard, make sacrifices and consistently follow your goals. And once you achieve wealth, take stock of the situation:
- Your past
- Your present
- Your future
- What is your worth—financially, spiritually, personally
- What will be your future journey/strategy

Once you are ready with this, you are also ready to take advice for your future plan.

Advice can come from many sources, and sometimes from the least expected sources, so develop a skill to listen actively and carefully. One of my clients used to tell me that he appointed various advisors, and carefully listened to their advices but did exactly the opposite and yet succeeded! Isn't it strange? It means that you should also learn to take in what is not being said. Don't follow any advice blindly.

When you achieve wealth, selecting a trustworthy advisor is crucial. Look for someone with a solid reputation, experience and expertise in financial matters. Ensure they align with your financial goals and get transparency in everything, including their fees. Review the financial plan regularly and be involved in the decision-making.

Don't hesitate before taking a second opinion if you have any doubts. Building a strong communicative relationship with your advisor is a must. Your advisor should be capable enough to help you navigate through the financial complexities of wealth management.

Here is a short checklist to help you find the right advisor for wealth planning:
- Credential and Qualifications
- Experience
- Reputation
- Following strict fiduciary duties
- Transparent Fees
- Client First Approach
- Availability
- Technology Integration
- Balancing Conflict Of Interest
- Following All Regulatory Compliances
- Good Client Retention Rate
- Network Of Professionals
- Risk Tolerance Assessment
- Good Ethical Standards
- Abreast with the latest trends
- Success Stories
- Exit Strategy

Evaluate based on the above points and select a financial advisor who aligns with your ethics and financial goals. You will need multiple experts as wealth management requires skilled expertise in various fields, such as investing, taxation, succession, legal etc.

In essence, financial success is a journey, and a skilled advisor is the compass that guides you through the twist and turns of wealth building.

Doctrine 97

Don't Flaunt Your Wealth

YOU MUST HAVE noticed that when rich people flaunt, nobody likes it. The flashy cars, designer clothes, lavish parties, big fat weddings, big diamonds and heavy jewellery—all these attract envy, jealousy, criticism, and snobbery.

Wealth is much-coveted; we all want to have it and that's why we are reading this book. Getting rich is an achievement. But how you handle wealth is a bigger achievement.

One of my friends inherited a huge piece of land. He, along with his two brothers, got a good amount of money by selling and starting various real estate projects on that land. As they got a huge amount of money suddenly, it was difficult for them to handle. Among the three brothers, two bought expensive cars and villas, went on flashy foreign tours and did every other thing that showed-off their wealth. The other one, along with his son, observed how people laughed and criticised their pretentious ways. Unlike the other two brothers, they learnt a hard lesson and decided to live a decent and sober life. They planned a good life, but with sensible spending. And what came out of all the show-off? Soon, the two brothers started struggling with their money.

Be careful with your money. Instead of showing-off your wealth, be discreet, tasteful, refined, and cultured. Be the person people find inspiring. Set a good example for all those young aspiring people.

Don't ever mention your worth. I know a business person who keeps calculating his income by years, months, hours and even seconds, and telling everyone he meets. The result was that people stopped meeting him and tried to avoid him as much as possible for all he ever did was show-off his wealth.

Remember, if you flaunt your wealth you will attract unwanted attention which can potentially make you a target for theft or scams. Also, displaying excessive wealth may create envy and resentment among others, leading to a strained relationship. Instead, practicing humility and modesty fosters a more positive and respectful environment.

Showcasing wealth doesn't necessarily correlate with personal happiness or fulfilment. Being discreet about your wealth helps maintain personal safety and fosters positive relationships allowing for a more balanced and fulfilling life.

One thing to remember always is that true wealth lies not in the display of possessions but in the richness of humility, kindness, and genuine connections.

Doctrine 98

Charitable Giving Versus Impact Investing

SINCE YOU WANT to share your wealth for the charity, you should know the new global trend—Impact Investing.

Charitable giving and impact investing are distinct concepts, but there is an emerging approach called Impact Philanthropy that seeks to blend elements of both charitable giving and impact investing.

Let's understand in details:

- **Charitable Giving:**

    Charitable giving involves donating money, resources, or time to nonprofit organisations without expecting financial returns.

    The primary goal for this is to address social, humanitarian, or environmental issues and make a positive impact on society.

    Donors may get tax benefits or deduction as per the prevailing rules.

- **Impact Investing:**
Impact investing aims to generate both financial returns and measurable positive social or environmental impact. Investors actively seek opportunities that align with their values, supporting business or projects that contribute to social and environmental well-being.

Though the financial returns are below the market rate, they reflect a willingness to prioritise impact alongside profits.
- **Impact Philanthropy—Blending Charitable Giving and Impact Investing:**
Impact philanthropy combines the principles of charitable giving with the strategic approach of impact investing.

Donors strategically invest their funds in projects or organisations that address societal challenges.

Philanthropists can make PRIs—Programme Related Investments or MRIs—Mission Related Investments. The investment can be done in social enterprises such as those focused on renewable energy, fair trade, or healthcare. The investment can be done in Community Development Financing too, such as affordable housing projects.

Balancing financial returns with social impact goals requires careful consideration. It involves accepting lower financial returns for greater societal benefits.

The latest trend gives you options to do charity with moderate returns. There are various area in which such investments can be done:
- Crisis Response
- Environmental Stewardship

- Educational Initiatives
- Access to Technology
- CSR
- Philanthropy
- Fair Trade Practices

A global perspective on sharing and giving wealth involves a multifaceted approach, encompassing economic policies, corporate practices, individual philanthropy, and collaborative efforts to address systemic issues and promote sustainable development on a worldwide scale.

Doctrine 99

Why You Should Share Your Wealth

WHEN YOU HAVE accumulated enough wealth, a part of it should be shared. Sharing wealth can lead to a more equitable society with reduced poverty and enhanced overall well-being. It fosters social stability, promotes education and healthcare access, and helps address systematic inequalities, creating a more sustainable and harmonious community.

Let's look at this in details:

- **Reducing Poverty:**
  By providing financial resources to those in need, the inequality issues can be resolved. This can lead to improved living conditions, better nutrition, and increased access to essential services.
- **Enhancing Education:**
  Shared wealth can find various educational initiatives such as scholarships. This helps break the cycle of poverty and contributes to creating more educated and skilled manpower.
- **Healthcare:**
  Wealth distribution can support healthcare infrastructure

and services, making medical care more accessible to a broader population.
- **Social Stability:**
Equal distribution of wealth can reduce social tensions and inequalities.
- **Fostering Innovations:**
Shared wealth can finance research and developments, encouraging innovation and technological advancements.
- **Creating a Stronger Middle Class:**
Wealth distribution that supports the middle class can lead to a more robust and resilient economy.
- **Building Social Capital:**
When wealth is shared, it can strengthen social bonds and community ties. This helps in creating a cohesive and resilient society.
- **Environmental Stewardship:**
Shared wealth can be directed towards sustainable practices and environmental efforts. This helps to develop a long-term ecological health that benefits the future generations.
- **Encouraging Philanthropy:**
Wealthy people sharing their wealth for good purpose inspires a culture of philanthropy, encouraging others to contribute to charitable causes.

Sharing wealth addresses not only immediate economic disparities but also contributes to the overall well-being and progress of society by promoting education, healthcare, innovations, and social cohesion. You will be lucky if you get an opportunity to share your wealth for a good purpose.

Doctrine 100

Legacy Wealth Sustainable Doctrines For Generations

WE ARE NOW on the last step of our journey—the journey which encompasses the various phases of money and wealth in a comprehensive guide for anyone who wants to understand money and various doctrines around wealth creation, preservation and sharing.

I have tried to make it as simple as possible, covering all aspects of wealth creation.

In this final doctrine, I am covering doctrines for wealth creation, not just for an individual. It focuses on creating a lasting impact for future generations, emphasising long-term financial strategies, ethical considerations, and the importance of education in preserving and growing family wealth.

Let's take a look on the doctrines of Legacy Wealth:

- **Multigenerational Planning:**
  Explore the significance of thinking beyond one's lifetime and developing strategies that can withstand economic fluctuations.
  Discuss estate planning, trust, and other tools that

facilitate a smooth transfer of wealth to successive generations.
- **Values and Ethics:**
  Emphasise the importance of instilling a strong set of values and ethical principles in managing wealth.
  Teach integrity, social responsibility, and sustainable practices to future generations. This helps them to achieve not only financial success but also create a positive impact on society.
- **Educational Investments:**
  Stress the role of education as a cornerstone for building and maintaining wealth.
  Encourage investing in the education of family members to empower them with the knowledge and skills needed to make informed financial decisions.
- **Entrepreneurial Mindset:**
  Discuss fostering an entrepreneurial mindset with the family, encouraging innovations, adaptability, and a proactive approach to wealth creation.
  This can involve supporting family members in pursuing their entrepreneurial ventures.
- **Diversification and Risk Management:**
  Reinforce the importance of diversification in investment and implementing effective risk management strategies to protect family's wealth over a long-term.
- **Philanthropy and Giving Back:**
  Explore the benefits of incorporating philanthropy into wealth management, emphasising the positive impact of giving back to communities and causes. Discuss creating a family philanthropy plan that aligns with the family values.

- **Adapting to Change:**
  Acknowledge the dynamic nature of the economic and social landscape and stress the need for adaptability. Encourage the family to stay informed about market trends, technological advancements, and global changes that could impact their wealth.

This is a comprehensive guide for not only accumulating wealth but also ensuring its enduring impact on future generations, fostering a legacy of financial success, responsibility, and positive contributions to society.

So remember that if you are able to create wealth, and I am sure you can by following these doctrines, share your wealth for a good cause as that's the real use for your wealth.

Wishing you a happy journey to create wealth!